D1527484

MY VIEW FROM 20 ROWS UP

One Pirate Fan's Story of ECU Football

Carl Davis

Foreword by Jeff Charles

For more information about book sales or the *Carl and Martha Davis Access Scholarship*, contact Carl Davis at carldavis.nc@gmail.com.

ISBN-13: 979-8-36-990838-9

Editor, Bethany Bradsher

Cover design and layout by Stephanie Whitlock Dicken.

Table of Contents

ECU Athletics

Foreword

By Jeff Charles, "The Voice of the Pirates"

Carl Davis is the epitome of a great Pirate fan. He literally bleeds purple and gold. His love affair for Pirate athletics and ECU began in the 1970s as a student. Through the decades his unwavering support of Pirate student-athletes, coaches and administrators has been a great example for all of Pirate Nation to follow. Through thirty years of following ECU football to almost every game, home or away, Carl has proven his loyalty to his favorite team and collected a range of colorful stories along the way. This book will spark memories for the fellow Pirate fans who shared the ups and downs of ECU games over those decades, and it will enrich the history of newer members of the Pirate Nation who haven't experienced the richness of the rivalries, triumphs and challenges that have paved the way to this point.

Carl has been a wonderful loyal friend to many, always willing to extend a helping hand to Pirates everywhere. I have always enjoyed seeing Carl on the dozens of road trips we have experienced together. It is those road trips that have provided a lifetime of memories and great stories, many of which you will experience in these pages. Whether the Pirates win or lose,

Carl has always been a positive beacon for everything ECU, and he has given his time and energy as a Pirate ambassador to help enrich the program. Fans like Carl are the backbone of ECU football. Thank you, Carl, for always being there; you are appreciated more than we can ever put into words.

Carl Davis

Preface

For many years, I have been passionate about East Carolina football. I am certainly not unique in that passion, but I have been very fortunate to follow Pirate athletics to many interesting venues and meet lots of players, coaches and family members, as well as both opposing fans and Pirate fans like me.

For more than two decades my wife and I have only missed attending, in person, four ECU football games anywhere the Pirates played. Starting in 1997 and continuing until the pandemic began, we traveled more than 190,000 miles supporting ECU Pirate football. It was an interesting experience and I learned things like how our opponents feel about East Carolina and what the fan experience is like at different universities.

One important thing has changed over the years: East Carolina's opponents now compete at a much higher level. We have often been defined by our opponents, and that's why many of the chapters in this book are categorized by the schools we have faced. Like ECU, many of these programs had a modest start. Some had very few fans and were an afterthought in their cities. I have tried to show how and why some of this has happened. Some programs have made tremendous progress—

from being almost invisible on their campus to playing in the College Football Playoff.

After all these games and all these people, there are some who stand out and are special for different reasons. I have devoted several chapters to those folks. Some of them will be familiar, and some will be people you don't know.

I believe very strongly that we need to remember our history. That's why I nominated Clarence Stasavich for the East Carolina Honorary Alumni Award in 2010, because he changed ECU football like no one before him. Steve Logan did much to make the football program what it is today, which is why I nominated him for the ECU Athletics Hall of Fame.

I must thank my wife, known to many as the "long-suffering" Martha Davis. She has endured heat, cold, rain, and snow as well as long drives, long plane rides, and countless hotel rooms. Her perspective about some of the people we have met over the years has been very valuable. I also need to thank my college roommate and still-best friend, Tom Peeler. Tom and his wife Jayne have joined us for many of the trips and games. His perspective, and especially his sense of humor, have helped make this journey such fun. We have been able to turn many of those football trips into mini-vacations. Our paths crossed with many, many Pirates not related to the actual games.

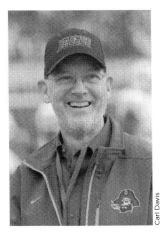
Carl Davis

A Pirate Fan for Life

With more than sixty years of Pirate football in my past, much of what has made it special didn't happen on the field. Some of the most memorable people I've encountered, in fact, haven't been players at all.

One good example is a man who sat near us for several decades. He would walk up the steps very close to our seats. Besides being the unofficial cheerleader for our section, this man would go out of the stadium at halftime of every game at Dowdy-Ficklen Stadium. When he returned early in the third quarter, he would always have several beers tucked, not so discreetly, under his shirt. As the years went on, he would bring in more and more beer. We marveled at his ability to get that much beer in through the gate and past security, which for us always seemed fairly tight. Finally, several years ago, early in the third quarter of a home game, I looked up and saw him coming up the stairs. There was water from melting ice pouring out of the sleeve of his rolled-up jacket, and a complete twelve-pack of beer was plainly visible. Good job, Pirate Fan!

MY VIEW FROM 20 ROWS UP

Pirates Face Number Two Club In The Nation

Nov. 5, 1959 East Carolinian

In The Beginning

With the success of the last thirty-plus years, many Pirate fans are unaware of the very humble beginnings of East Carolina football. With the notable exception of Appalachian State and one game each at Southern Miss and Virginia Tech, ECU did not play a single opponent that is currently in FBS football (Division I-A) between 1932, when ECU football began, and 1963. That is not to say that East Carolina didn't play good football for the first three decades, but that there were very few of what most fans would consider quality big-name opponents.

I didn't start as an East Carolina fan. Growing up in Hickory, my family didn't follow ECU and we didn't know any ECU fans. In fact, we were the enemy. It was hard not to be a Lenoir-Rhyne fan, since it was the local school which has always had a significant grip on the community.

My father started college at what was then North Carolina State College, until World War II and twenty months as a POW guest of the Germans in what is now Poland got in the way of his education. After the war, he returned to Hickory and finished his college career at Lenoir-Rhyne. My mother worked during the war building B-26 bombers in Baltimore and returned to Hickory and earned a two-year degree at LR.

13

For the first five years of my life, we lived right down the street from Lenoir-Rhyne. We were one block from campus and three blocks from what was then called College Field, home of the LR Bears. College Field was also the home field for Hickory High School, since the high school didn't have a football field with bleachers.

We even went to church at St. Andrews Lutheran Church across the street from campus. St. Andrews was officially affiliated with Lenoir-Rhyne and since LR was a Lutheran college, many students, staff, and faculty attended services there.

My family was even involved in helping build the college. My paternal grandfather, Garland Davis, worked for the company that built Shuford Gymnasium and P.E. Monroe Auditorium on campus. He and my paternal grandmother also lived in the LR neighborhood and were involved with the college community. In a small town like Hickory, it's hard not to be involved with the only college in the community.

The football tradition at Lenoir-Rhyne is a long one starting in 1907, but it all centered around one man—Clarence Stasavich. To say that Coach Stas was the most popular man in Catawba County in the late '50s would be an understatement. He was a tall and very handsome man. Everyone loves a winner, and Stas was a winner.

Coach Stas grew up in Illinois but had gone to college and played football at Lenoir-Rhyne in the 1930s. After World War II, he came back and became the head coach in 1946, staying until 1961. His 121-37-6 record at LR made him a celebrity in this small Southern town. His 121 wins are still the most in LR history. After losing the NAIA National Championship game in 1959, the Bears under Stas came back to the championship game and won it all in 1960. Lenoir-Rhyne went to five bowl games under Coach Stas and has not been back to a bowl since 1960. They have only played in the Division II playoffs once since 1962.

The current LR football guide labels the 1955-1962 period as "The Glory Days." It is easy to see why he was such a favorite.

To understand Lenoir-Rhyne it is important to understand the city of Hickory. Unlike many other North Carolina cities in the '50s, Hickory was not very reliant on agriculture. In the postwar era, Hickory was a leading center for manufacturing furniture and textiles. More than other places at that time, Hickory had a much higher percentage of two income earners in a family. That seemed to carry over to boost education, the arts, and of course, sports.

Hickory High had a long football tradition as well. The legendary coach Frank Barger is still the third winningest coach in North Carolina High School football history, with 273 wins in thirty-five seasons. There was an obvious player pipeline from Hickory High to LR, and the other local schools heavily fed LR as well.

Logistically there was also a connection. The original Hickory High (Claremont Central) was built in the downtown part of Hickory and only had a football practice field with no bleachers. Since it was four blocks from College Field at Lenoir-Rhyne, all the Hickory High home games were played there. HHS basketball was played at LR in Shuford Gym on campus. It seemed to be a good relationship for both the high school and the college. If you lived in Hickory, you were probably attached to Lenoir-Rhyne in some way—either directly or through the high school.

In the 1950s, television in western North Carolina didn't offer much sports programming. There was major league baseball on Saturdays and the NFL on Sundays. The Washington Redskins were the only NFL option, but that was not a problem because the Redskins were North Carolina's team in that era. Since there were no pro sports teams in the major sports, the Redskins, who appeared on TV on Sundays, were the football choice by default. Television was my only football exposure until my grandfather stepped in.

My maternal grandfather, MT Reavis, is the one who introduced me to college football and helped me learn about the game. He is responsible for guiding me in life and for many good things besides college football.

My mother and I moved in with my grandparents after my parents divorced, and in many ways my grandfather acted as my father. He certainly did when it came to discipline! MT Reavis enjoyed Lenoir-Rhyne football, particularly when the team was winning. And in the late 50s, of course, that was most of the time.

We would attend most of the home games at College Field and an occasional away game at Guilford, Appalachian or Catawba College. Those were always fun times. In those old stadiums, you were always close to the field and close to the action. In the days without a large video screen and instant replay, you had to pay attention and have a good memory! There was much to entertain a preteen boy in the '50s. It was loud, and the sights and sounds made it exciting. You had bands, great food like hot dogs, and football right in front of you. What could be better? There was just something almost magical about Saturday nights with the bright white lines on freshly mowed grass under the stadium lights.

In the 1959 season, my grandfather proposed that we travel to Greenville to follow the Bears as they took on East Carolina College. That was not an easy trip in 1959, or even ten years later when I made the trip to start my freshman year. It was more than seven long hours passing through Winston-Salem, Greensboro, Durham, Raleigh and more than a dozen smaller towns— a long ride to see a football game. This was always a hard-fought game, and the Bears still hold a 15-6 overall record with EC.

November 7, 1959 was my first East Carolina game, and I will always remember it for a number of reasons. First, it was my first overnight road game. Second, my whole family was there, including my mother and grandparents. Third, Lenoir-Rhyne won and the long trip was worth it!

For East Carolina and Lenoir-Rhyne, this was a memorable game in a number of ways. The Bears went on to play for the NAIA National Championship four games later in the Holiday Bowl, and their loss in the National Championship game was their only loss of the year. It turned out to be their only loss in two seasons. For East Carolina it was memorable because of the way the game ended. It was one of those "last play of the game" scenarios.

In 1959, East Carolina College played football in College Stadium. It would be four seasons later that Ficklen Stadium welcomed Wake Forest for the first game in the current location. College Stadium, located on the main campus near 10th Street, is also known to have hosted presidential candidate John F. Kennedy less than a year later in September 1960.

The game was memorable to East Carolina College fans for the wrong reason. First of all, Lenoir-Rhyne was ranked the number-two small college team in the country. Secondly, the Pirates led until very late in the game. It was a good game for James Speight, who had his number 29 retired at East Carolina, and future Buffalo Bill and NC Sports Hall of Fame member Glenn Bass. Unfortunately for Speight and Bass, though, their great performances were negated when LR scored with just 21 seconds remaining in the game to make it 21-20 in favor of the Pirates. Like Steve Logan forty years later, Coach Stasavich didn't kick the extra point but went for the two-point conversion. Lenoir-Rhyne tailback Lee Farmer was apparently stopped at the five-yard line by EC's Sonny Basinger and future ECU head coach Ed Emory. According to EC coach Jack Boone, the whistle blew and then Lee Farmer threw a desperation lateral into the endzone that was caught by Marcus Midgett. Coach Boone also claimed that there were linemen downfield on the forward lateral.

The East Carolinian's headline the next day said, "Decision Robs EC's Pirates of Upset Over Bears." Another paper said, "We Were Robbed." Lenoir-Rhyne's local hometown paper, The Hickory Daily Record, said that there was a moment of "uncertainty." East Carolina Coach Jack Boone vigorously protested, receiving a 15-yard penalty for his efforts. Later he even wrote a letter to the group that assigned officials for the game. Fans poured onto the field. Considering that the game was also a muddy mess and the players' numbers were totally obscured, it was the perfect ending! That was my introduction to Greenville and East Carolina Pirate football.

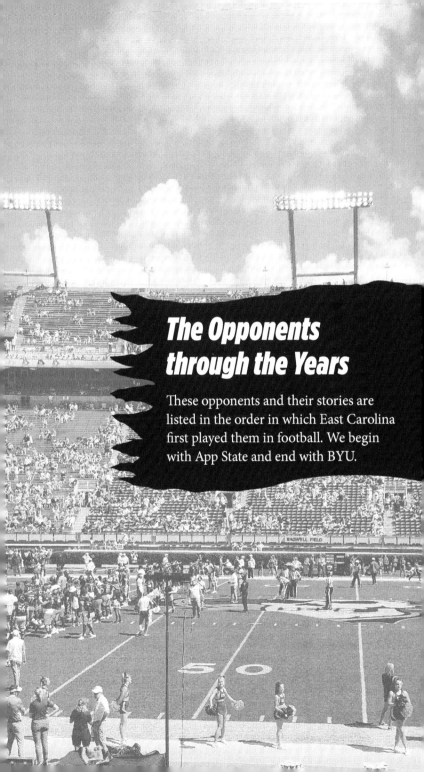

The Opponents through the Years

These opponents and their stories are listed in the order in which East Carolina first played them in football. We begin with App State and end with BYU.

MY VIEW FROM 20 ROWS UP

Appalachian State University (App State)

This series started in 1932 and continued for 89 years, with a total of thirty-two games played through 2021. Like East Carolina and so many colleges, Appalachian began as a teachers college. For many years, App State could be characterized as the best of FCS. Much of that success could be attributed to longtime coach Jerry Moore. He coached at App State for twenty-four years and is the winningest coach in App State and Southern Conference history. His teams won ten Southern Conference championships and three consecutive FCS (formerly D-1AA) national championships. Moore's Mountaineer teams only faced the Pirates twice near the end of his career, and ECU won both games.

ECU and App State met for the first time in 1932, ECU's inaugural year of football. The Pirates never scored and they lost 21-0. In fact the Pirates didn't score in any games in 1932. App State would go on to win the first ten games in this series, but the Pirates would finally break through in 1952, defeating the Mountaineers 22-19, and they actually won three games in the early 1950s. The next six games were all won by App State, but that changed when Clarence Stasavich arrived in Greenville in 1962. At that point, App State led the football series 17-4.

While the series stopped for thirty years from 1979 to 2009, the Pirates have dominated 9-3 since the arrival of Coach Stas in 1962. The Pirates left the Southern Conference after 1976 to become an independent and pursue D-1 football, while App State chose to remain in the Southern Conference until 2014 and then move to the Sun Belt Conference and FBS.

After thirty years, the series would resume in 2009. The Skip-Holtz-led Pirates were highly favored as both teams kicked off their seasons. The first half was all ECU. While the Pirate offense played well and scored often, it was the defense that played the best. App State could only generate one scoring drive in the first half and the Pirates would take a 27-7 lead into the dressing room. The third quarter was dominated by both defenses, but ECU got a safety after a nice punt pinned the Mountaineers inside the 3-yard line. The fourth quarter was all App State, with four possessions by the Pirates yielding only 32 yards and no points. The Mountaineers would put together three drives and score 17 points, but it wasn't enough. Despite the fourth quarter comeback, the Pirates held on 29-24.

Three years later in 2012, the Mountaineers returned to Dowdy-Ficklen Stadium to open the season. App State scored first but the Pirates answered and led 14-10 at the half. A Mountaineer field goal closed the gap to 14-13, but a 90-yard kickoff return by Lance Ray turned it all ECU purple. The Pirates would score twice more and go on to win 35-13.

The most recent game in the series came in Charlotte at Bank of America Stadium to open the 2021 season. After both teams exchanged punts, the Pirates got an electric 65-yard scoring pass from Holton Ahlers to Keaton Mitchell. Other than two field goals, that's all the scoring the Pirates could manage until the final minutes of the game. Bad penalties by the Pirates and solid play by the Mountaineers ended in a 33-19 win for App State. They would go on to win the Sun Belt

Conference and finish with a 10-4 record.

App State leads the series 20-12, but that really doesn't tell the story of the last ninety years. While ECU chose to leave the Southern Conference, Appalachian remained and became a force in FCS football. The transition to FBS and the Sun Belt took only two years of adjustment but the Mountaineers are right back again, having won five of the last six conference championships.

SOUTHERN MISS

VS

$45

Coach Logan
1992-2002

SATURDAY
October 19, 2013
DOWDY-FICKLEN STADIUM
No Readmittance   Date Subject to Change   No Refunds

Location	Gate
South	**2-3**
6	V	*1
Section	Row	Seat

91429222927468

GATE
8

SECTION
P

ROW
3

2006 NCAA FOOTBALL
SOUTHERN MISS
vs.
EAST CAROLINA
M.M. ROBERTS STADIUM
SAT. OCT. 28, 7:00 P
$29.00
NO REFUNDS NO EXCHANGES

Location		Gate
South		**2-3**
6	V	*1
Section	Row	Seat

Pirates

EAST CAROLINA
VS

ECU

SATURDAY, NOV. 5, 2011
DOWDY-FICKLEN STADIUM
No Readmittance   Date Subject to Change   No Refunds

91430918481727

Location	Gate
	2-3
South	*1
6	V	Seat
Section	Row	

The University of Southern Mississippi (USM)

East Carolina has played the University of Southern Mississippi more than any other school in history, first playing Southern Miss in 1951, the year I was born. The Pirates have had minimal success against the Golden Eagles with an overall 12-27 record. Even though one USM website ranks ECU at the top of a list of their rivals, most ECU fans would probably not consider Southern Miss as one of their top rivals. Even so, for many of those years USM and ECU have had a somewhat parallel existence. The years in Conference USA together strengthened the bond between the two schools that began a generation before that.

USM has been labeled, correctly or not, as a "directional" school. Like ECU and UNC-CH, the in-state flagship university, Ole Miss, avoided playing Southern Miss for many years. Like ECU with NCSU, they had a little more success scheduling Mississippi State. Again, like their ECU counterparts, the Golden Eagles have a chip on their shoulders, and they proudly show it. Years ago, the words "ANYONE, ANYWHERE, ANYTIME" were printed on the grass at the 20-yard line for all to see. And they meant it. They often took three-for-one or four-for-one deals with larger and more prominent schools like

Alabama, Auburn, Florida, Florida State and Nebraska. They won some of those games and even with three- or four-for-one, they found it hard to get prominent teams to play them. If any school has a chip on their shoulder, it's Southern Miss. Like with ECU, this is not such a bad thing.

Also like ECU, the Southern Miss fans are very genuine and very loyal. They take great pride in their football program. In terms of tailgating, they are the most welcoming of any group I have ever encountered. When you walk through a Southern Miss tailgate area wearing a purple shirt, dozens of folks will welcome you and offer you food and drink. We met Pro Football Hall of Famer Ray Guy. We met the lieutenant governor. We met the president of the university. All of them welcomed ECU fans like they were their friends and neighbors. The USM mindset appears to be that we share a common bond. I'm not sure that ECU fans know or understand this.

While we share a common past, East Carolina and Southern Mississippi are different in a number of ways as well. First, North Carolina is a more populous, more urban, and more economically advantaged state than our southern counterpart. Second, ECU has a well-developed and very successful health sciences program with a long-standing medical school, dental school and large affiliated hospital. These two things differentiate the schools, but the agricultural region, the history, and the culture definitely make the people seem very similar.

Hattiesburg has about half the population of Greenville. The university, like in Greenville, is the center of the community. As you drive through Hattiesburg, it is hard not to see similarities.

Our first visit to Hattiesburg and Southern Mississippi was during Thanksgiving weekend in 2000. After the weekend, most of the people in our group called it the Mud Bowl. It rained hard all the way from New Orleans to Hattiesburg. When we arrived at the stadium, it was literally raining so hard you could barely see across the field. Southern Miss, at that time, had a natural grass field that barely covered the black Mississippi soil. The field drainage was very poor, and hours of rain had caused water to pond all over, especially along the sidelines. The entire ECU sideline was covered in six inches of water.

On the opening kickoff Keith Stokes got a good return, but when he was tackled along the ECU sideline, as he slid forward he actually created a wake in the water. From that point forward, his name and number were covered in mud and were completely unreadable. Within five minutes, every other player's number was unreadable, too.

The game was a tight one, and in those muddy conditions it was as low scoring as you would expect. ECU linebacker Greg LeFever picked off a Jeff Kelley pass near midfield and started sloshing toward the endzone. Long before he could get there, he fumbled in the mud. Fortunately for the Pirates, defensive back Kelly Hardy was trailing the play. Hardy picked up the ball out of the mud and scored. The Pirate defense was tested, but held and the Pirates won the "Mud Bowl" 14-9 over a very good Southern Miss team.

Several years after the Hattiesburg mudfest, the outcome in Greenville against the Golden Eagles was not as good because of the dominant Southern Miss defense. The 2001 season was a year of ups and downs. The Pirates were 5-4 coming into the game and David Garrard was having a great year, but that day ECU fumbled four times and Southern Miss recovered all four. Late in the game while driving for what could have been the winning score, Garrard threw an interception to Rod Davis. Davis was a great linebacker who later played for the Vikings and Panthers in the NFL. Garrard never saw him, and that pick sealed the game 28-21 in favor of the Golden Eagles.

A game I didn't see between ECU and USM helped change the rules of college football forever. In 1986 in Greenville,

Southern Miss was trailing 24-23. On the last play of the game, the Golden Eagles threw a Hail Mary followed by an illegal forward lateral. At that time, a game couldn't end on a penalty, so after marking off the penalty, they kicked a field goal and won the game 26-24. It was a tough loss for the Pirates. The current rules say that a penalty on the offensive team will not extend the game. In other words, Southern Miss would not have had a chance at a field goal.

For twenty-nine years, eighteen of them as head coach, Jeff Bower walked the sidelines at Southern Miss. He had been a quarterback for the Golden Eagles and an assistant. He was named Coach of the Decade by Conference USA. His last fourteen seasons as head coach each produced a winning record, but he was fired at the end of the 2007 season—proving that sometimes winning is just not enough in college football. Bower was replaced by Larry Fedora. He coached the Golden Eagles for four seasons before leaving for North Carolina after the 2011 season. It was under Fedora that I saw my most memorable ECU matchup with Southern Miss.

In 2010, I was trying to get a new alumni center off the ground at ECU. In the process, I was visiting alumni centers around the country. I took the opportunity to visit a very impressive renovation that had been done to the original USM President's house to create a novel but nice alumni center facility. Paul Clifford, ECU Vice Chancellor for Advancement and President of the ECU Alumni Association, had connected me with his counterpart at Southern Miss. The alumni director gave my wife and me an excellent tour, answered all our questions and really was most welcoming. After the tour we tailgated again with the Southern Miss fans. It was their homecoming, so there was an extra buzz in the air.

The game started poorly for the Pirates. In fact, Southern Miss scored on their first four possessions and led 20-0 after the first quarter. The Pirates rallied back and were aided by an 87-yard kick return for a touchdown by Jonathan Williams. Dominique Davis had a good game in spite of three interceptions, one of which was returned for a touchdown. He still holds the ECU single-season touchdown passing record. At the end it came down to fourth and seven when Davis connected for a 32-yard score to Michael Bowman and the Pirates came back to win 44-43. The funny part was an email from Paul Clifford to his USM colleague. It said, "At first I was insulted that Southern Miss had chosen to play the Pirates as a homecoming opponent, but when I watched the first quarter, I understood why. I turned off the TV before the second quarter. How much did y'all win by?"

Virginia Tech

East Carolina's history with Virginia Tech really began in 1987 and continued every year until the mid-1990's. Since then the two schools have played thirteen times. The actual rivalry began in 1956 at Mitchell Field in Bluefield, West Virginia. Virginia Tech played several "home" games there in the '30s, '40s and '50s. The game with ECC in 1956 was the last time the Hokies played in Bluefield.

Beginning in 1987, the two teams met every year for the next eight seasons with an equal number of games split between Greenville and Blacksburg. Those eight games were split evenly with the Pirates and the Hokies each winning four games. There seemed to be parity between East Carolina and Virginia Tech during most of those years.

Prior to 1991 Virginia Tech, like ECU, was an independent. Joining the Big East in 1991 provided a step up for the Hokies. With more money from the BCS and some new rivals like Miami, Temple, and Boston College, Virginia Tech began to rise in prominence. While these were not natural rivals, they were also up-and-coming teams. With neighbor and longtime rival West Virginia also in the Big East, the Hokies were able to successfully recruit against their neighbor Virginia and many schools in North Carolina.

In 1987, Frank Beamer came from Murray State to coach at Tech. Beamer was a former Hokie player, and he stayed for twenty-eight years with great success. His record against the Pirates in those years would be 12-7. In 2018 he was elected to the College Football Hall of Fame and a statue was erected in his honor at Lane Stadium.

While the 22-game football rivalry was certainly significant, the game in Blacksburg on September 1, 2007 had a special meaning. It was the first game following the April shooting at Virginia Tech that left thirty-two people dead and a campus and nation in shock. It is the deadliest school shooting in U.S. history, and at the time it was also the deadliest mass shooting in U.S. history. ESPN brought College Gameday to Blacksburg to begin the season as a way for the sports world to help in the healing process. Prior to the game, there were several ceremonies in remembrance of the victims of the shooting. Thirty-two orange balloons were released symbolizing the thirty-two victims while a video played. To say that 67,000 people were in tears would not accurately describe the emotion of that moment. It was much more than that. Those at Lane Stadium that afternoon will never forget it.

ECU Chancellor Steve Ballard and Director of Athletics Terry Holland presented a check for $100,000 to the Hokie Hope Fund, with Pirates from all over the country contributing to this donation. After the presentation, the Virginia Tech fans started a cheer back and forth across the stadium, "Thank You --- Pirates." It's hard to imagine two universities could be more connected than at that moment. This was the ultimate show of sportsmanship. After the emotion before the game, the Pirates took a 7-3 lead in the second quarter on a short Chris Johnson run. An interception return for a touchdown later in the quarter gave the Hokies a 10-7 halftime margin. Tech got another touchdown in the fourth quarter to make the final score 17-7. The Pirates came into the game as a 27.5-point underdog, but that day it was really about much more than the game.

In the past two decades, Virginia Tech holds a 12-3 record over the Pirates. The last two games in 2016 and 2017 were blowout losses, but 2011 and 2013, both played in Greenville, were close one-score losses that could have gone either way. Typical of those games was a 2000 Michael-Vick-led Hokie team that defeated the Pirates, led by David Garrard, 45-28 in Dowdy Ficklen Stadium. For most Pirate fans, there have been three truly memorable games since 1992.

In the special 2014 season, Ruffin McNeill led the Pirates to Blacksburg to face the No. 17 ranked Hokies. Shane Carden threw three touchdown passes in the first quarter and the Pirates seemed on their way to a win. Three straight trips to the red zone in the second quarter yielded no points for ECU, so the halftime score was 21-7. Two late touchdowns by the Hokies, including one with just 1:20 remaining, tied the score. Carden engineered a three-play, 65-yard drive and scored on a one-yard dive with 16 seconds remaining. The Pirates won for the first time since 1991 in Blacksburg, prevailing 28-21. It was the first win by the Pirates over a ranked team on the road in eighteen years.

After three good seasons, 2015 was not a great year for East Carolina football. The highlight of the year was the game in Greenville with the Hokies. A crowd of more than 50,000 saw Tech take a 14-0 lead early in the game and the Pirates answer with two touchdowns. The score was 14-14 at the end of the first quarter. The Pirates used a two-quarterback system that day. The last three touchdowns came from James Summers, who threw for one touchdown and ran for two others. In the end, Summers' 169 yards rushing made the difference. The Hokies simply were not prepared to stop the running ECU quarterback. Tech got a late touchdown, but the Pirates won the game by a final score of 35-28.

For most East Carolina fans, the most memorable game with Virginia Tech came over Labor Day weekend in 2008 at Bank of America Stadium in Charlotte. The Hokies were ranked No. 17 in the country. The Skip-Holtz-coached Pirates were riding high after finishing the season with an emotional win over Boise State in the Hawaii Bowl. The crowd of more than 72,000 was fairly evenly divided between the Pirate and Hokie fans. At the time, it was the largest regular season college football attendance in North Carolina history.

The game started slowly with neither team scoring in the first quarter. The second quarter saw two ECU fumbles turn into two Tech touchdowns. The Pirates fought back after a Nick Johnson interception and scored their first touchdown to make it 14-7 in favor of the Hokies at halftime. In the third quarter, a Patrick Pinkney pass made it 14-13. Virginia Tech, known for great special teams play, blocked the extra point and returned it for two points to make the score 16-13 Tech. Another Hokie score on the first play of the fourth quarter made it 22-13 after the extra point missed the mark. With only 3:36 remaining in the game, Patrick Pinkney would end a 73-yard drive with a touchdown. The Pirate defense held, and with only 1:16 left the Hokies were forced to punt from their own territory. In one of the most exciting moments in ECU football history, T.J. Lee broke through the Hokie line, blocked the punt, scooped up the ball and scored from 27 yards out. While the Pirate fans celebrated, the Virginia Tech fans were stunned. The Hokies and Coach Beamer, who for many years had used special teams play to win games, were defeated on a special teams play by Skip Holtz and the Pirates. The final score was 27-22.

The expression "all good things must come to an end" was illustrated in 2018 when Hurricane Florence hit Eastern

North Carolina. Maybe it should actually be "no good deed goes unpunished." On Tuesday, September 11, 2018, ECU announced that it would not travel to Blacksburg and play No. 13 ranked Virginia Tech. The game was scheduled for four days after the announcement. At the time of the announcement, Hurricane Florence was a strong Category Four storm with 140 mph winds off the Atlantic coast. It was predicted to come ashore in North Carolina and pass directly over Greenville with 130-mile-per-hour winds on Friday morning. Also, at the time of the announcement, there was a state of emergency declared for North and South Carolina and for Virginia. Greenville was under a hurricane watch.

The university took other precautions. Classes were canceled until the following week. The residence halls were evacuated by Wednesday morning. All athletic competitions in every sport, home and away, were canceled. The simple reason for these actions was experience. In 1999, Hurricane Floyd had devastated eastern North Carolina. The football team had traveled to South Carolina and became stranded due to the conditions. It was more than a week before the team could make it back to Greenville. Hurricane Mathew had a similar effect in 2016. Greenville and ECU understood the severity of the situation and took the actions they thought necessary. ECU was not alone in its actions. NC State canceled its game with No. 14 West Virginia that was scheduled to be played in Raleigh. UNC canceled its game with No. 18 UCF scheduled on the same day to be played in Chapel Hill. Virginia moved its home game with Ohio University to Nashville. Seven other college football games in the Carolinas and Virginia were either canceled or rescheduled. All of this happened the same day that East Carolina decided not to travel to Blacksburg.

Unfortunately, the administration in Blacksburg did not see eye-to-eye with the East Carolina administrators. Their statement was that they had hoped to wait another day to determine the weather conditions. Three months later, Virginia Tech Athletic Director Whit Babcock announced that the Hokies would not be coming to Greenville in the 2019 season as originally scheduled. He further stated that future games previously scheduled between East Carolina and Virginia Tech would be canceled. Eleven years after "Thank You --- Pirates" rang out from 67,000 fans in Lane Stadium, it was over.

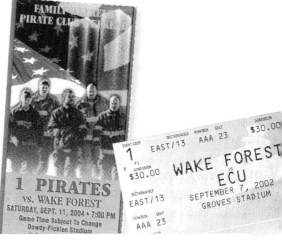

Wake Forest University

The expectations and the future of East Carolina football changed dramatically with a game against Wake Forest University. Prior to 1963, East Carolina College played its home games at College Field on Tenth Street, approximately where the Brewster Building is today. Leo Jenkins began a campaign to build a new stadium. The new Ficklen Memorial Stadium would seat 10,000 fans initially, with stands only originally built on the south side. Capacity was expanded to 20,000 a few years later with the addition of seating on the north side.

Wake Forest, although a small school in terms of enrollment, was one of the founding members of the Atlantic Coast Conference. Having the Demon Deacons come to Greenville to open the brand new Ficklen Stadium was a big deal. It's hard to know whether Leo Jenkins or new coach Clarence Stasavich was the catalyst for the deal. There was no return game to Winston Salem in this arrangement.

The Pirates had opened Coach Stasavich's second season with a loss on the road at Richmond 10-7. The game in the new stadium was played at night before 17,000 excited fans. Temporary seats had been brought in on the north side. The Pirates led at the half 12-10. ECC halfback Tom Michel scored three touchdowns in the "versatile single wing offense" and East Carolina got its first win in the new stadium over Wake Forest College 20-10. Michel would play one season in the NFL and later be elected to the East Carolina Athletics Hall of Fame. The team would finish a great season 9-1 with a win in the Northeastern Bowl.

The teams would not meet again until 1979 in Winston-Salem. This was Coach Pat Dye's sixth and final year at ECU. The game was tied at 13 at the half. With the Deacons up 23-20, Vern Davenport attempted a 54-yard field goal which fell short, and the Deacons held on for an upset win.

It would be 18 years before ECU again played Wake Forest. This was the Demon Deacons' second trip to Greenville after opening the new stadium in 1963. This time it was Coach Steve Logan leading the Pirates. Wake Forest took a commanding 21-0 lead in the second quarter and it looked like a blowout for the Deacs. For the rest of the game, though, they would only get a field goal, as the ECU defense led by Rod Coleman and Dewayne Ledford took command. The Pirates scored the winning touchdown with 3:55 remaining in the game on a short pass to Scott Harley. An interception by the Pirates would end the game with the Pirates winning 25-24.

The series resumed in 2001 for the next five years. 2001 was the first year for new Wake Coach Jim Grobe, who would remain at Wake Forest for twelve years. His tenure at Wake would peak in 2006 with an 11-2 record and Wake's first ACC Championship in 36 years.

The next five games were not good ones for the Pirates. In 2001, in Grobe's first game at Wake Forest, the Deacs' running game proved very successful, as they piled up 290 yards on the ground in Dowdy-Ficklen stadium but started the game with a safety. The Pirates never led but David Garrard scored on a 10-yard run with under four minutes remaining in the game.

His rushing attempt for a two-point conversion failed, and the Pirates lost 21-19.

The next season in Winston-Salem, it was another slow start for the Pirates. Wake led 20-3 in the third quarter. ECU quarterback Paul Troth had four interceptions in the 27-22 loss. Statistically the two teams were almost even, but five turnovers versus one turnover made the difference for Wake Forest.

The final three games were similar. In 2003, early in the John Thompson era, five turnovers again were the undoing for the Pirates. The Pirates outgained the Demon Deacons but lost again 34-16. 2004 brought another loss to the Deacons. This time the score was 31-17. The only ECU highlight was an 84-yard touchdown run by freshman Chris Johnson. The final game with Wake Forest was in 2005 and was the first road game for new coach Skip Holtz. Unlike 2004, the highlights came from a different Chris. Wake's Chris Barclay ran for 210 yards and the Pirates were down 24-3 in the second quarter. There was no magic for ECU, and the final score was 44-34.

Although the series started well for the Pirates in 1963 on the opening day of Ficklen Stadium, it has been dominated by Wake Forest. Five of the six wins came under Coach Jim Grobe. His teams recruited solid defensive players and played good scoring defense. It's interesting to note that Grobe came to Wake from Ohio University, where he lost two games to the Pirates and Coach Steve Logan in 1996 and 1998.

University of Louisville

Like a lot of other schools, Louisville was in a much different position when East Carolina first joined Conference USA and the two schools started competing against each other. While ECU had played Louisville a few times in the '60s, starting in 1997 it became an almost-annual event.

For a school that was dominated by basketball and the intense rivalry with the University of Kentucky, Louisville developed a good football program rather quickly. This was due in part to John Schnatter, the founder of Papa John's Pizza. Schnatter, a Ball State alumnus from nearby Jeffersonville, Indiana, bought the naming rights to the new stadium for five million dollars when it opened in 1998. He later contributed another ten million. The quick rise in the pizza business and the location in a medium-sized city with no pro sports competition fueled the rise in Louisville football. ECU played Louisville in the old stadium in 1997 in front of fewer than 13,000 fans. Three years later when East Carolina returned to Louisville and played for the first time in Papa John's Stadium, it was in front of 38,000 fans.

Wisely, the University of Louisville built the stadium in an area that made sense for the program. It was near the old stadium but also close to Freedom Hall, the basketball arena, and the Kentucky Exposition Center. The entrance to Churchill Downs is also close to the stadium. They created a sports corridor and a sports destination, and the city embraced the University of Louisville and its football program.

Basketball didn't need any help. Coach Rick Pitino's team was always ranked and always competitive. Rick Pitino was a larger-than-life character. Pitino came to Louisville after coaching the New York Knicks, winning the NCAA Championship as the coach of Louisville's biggest rival, Kentucky, and coaching the Boston Celtics. In his sixteen years as the head coach at Louisville, he won two NCAA National Championships.

While the focus of this book is on football, it's important while discussing Louisville to mention Rick Pitino's first trip to Greenville to play the Pirates. It was an interesting one. For a school with very limited success in basketball like ECU, this was a big deal. The game was highly anticipated and ECU was a huge underdog. The night before the game, a group of ECU students came up with an interesting idea. It was rumored that Pitino wore a toupee on the back of his head. The students contacted a local carpet dealer who gave them old carpet remnants. They cut these in four-by-four inch squares and handed them out with bobby pins to students as they entered the arena. By game time, there were hundreds of students behind the Louisville bench with bright blue carpet squares on their heads. Pitino, always a showman, made his grand entrance about one minute before tipoff. The students held up a sign and shouted, "Hey Rick, we have our rugs, too!" Pitino laughed and pointed to the sign. To everyone's surprise, the Pirates won the game. The crowd made a difference. In the postgame interview, Pitino paid ECU fans a big compliment by saying it was the toughest crowd he had ever faced.

In football, the University of Louisville was an independent for many years. They were early members of Conference USA and took the first opportunity to move to a BCS conference in 2004 when they jumped to the Big East. Before the jump, they won three Conference USA championships under coaches John L. Smith and Bobby Petrino.

In Conference USA, the Pirates and Cardinals would meet seven times before Louisville left to join the Big East for the 2005 season. In those seven games, the Pirates could only manage two wins. Surprisingly, both of those wins came on the road, including the first time ECU played in the new Papa John's Stadium.

East Carolina first visited the new stadium for a nationally televised Thursday night game in 2000. Quarterback David Garrard had a good first half and the PIrates led 28-10 at halftime. What looked like an easy win for the Pirates turned into a competitive game, as Louisville's starting quarterback was injured and Mike Watkins replaced him. The Pirates never scored again, but the Pirate defense was just good enough. Four different ECU players had interceptions in the game, and on the final drive by the Cardinals the ball sailed wide right of future New England Patriot wide receiver and Super Bowl MVP Deion Branch. The Pirates ran out the clock and won 28-25.

After the first three games, the Cardinals, first under John L. Smith and later Bobby Petrino, seemed to create separation from the Pirates. ECU was outscored by Louisville 178 to 81 in those last four games. The much-improved football program and a long history of basketball success made Louisville a perfect fit for the Big East and a target when the ACC expanded.

My Louisville Travel Log:

Visited Churchill Downs and the Louisville Slugger Factory

$45

FRIDAY
November 23, 2012
DOWDY-FICKLEN STADIUM
No Readmittance   Date Subject to Change   No Refunds

Location		Gate
South		2-3
6	V	*1
Section	Row	Seat

9143283189214

MARSHALL

Location		Gate
South		2-3
6	V	4
Section	Row	Seat

4 PIRATES

SATURDAY, OCT. 23, 2010, 4:15PM
Dowdy-Ficklen Stadium

$40

Location		Gate
South		2-3
6	V	4
Section	Row	Seat

SEC
103
ROW
18
SEAT
3
FEES
$3.00
PRICE
$29.00

MARSHALL
vs
ECU
October 3, 2009
Saturday – 12:00pm
JOAN C. EDWARDS STADIUM

44

Marshall University

Not too many schools not named Notre Dame have Hollywood movies made about their football team, but Marshall was the subject of a major film, We Are Marshall, because of the deadliest sports tragedy in history. ECU and Marshall are forever bound by that tragedy in November, 1970. I attended that game, but time has taken a toll on my memory. I do remember hearing about the crash that night, and I remember the strange sinking feeling I had. I still get that feeling when the subject of the crash comes up again. The movie is definitely worth watching, but they took a few liberties with the ECU part.

The Thundering Herd and ECU began their series four years earlier in 1967. There are a number of parallels between the two mostly rural state-supported schools.

The Pirates and the Herd only played once in the next thirty years before the 2001 GMAC Bowl. That game was in Greenville in 1978, and it was a 45-0 ECU win. It was clear that Marshall was still rebuilding from the 1970 crash, which was a slow process. The most notable fact from that game was the linebacker who had 14 tackles for Marshall. It was a young player named Mike Hamrick. He would go on to become the athletic director at ECU and later return to his alma mater as the AD at Marshall.

In the early 1980s Marshall football began to flourish, competing very successfully in Division 1-AA (FCS). In the ten years from 1987-1996, the Herd played for the national championship six times, while winning two championships. They moved up to Division 1-A in 1997 and joined the Mid-American Conference.

The Pirates and the Herd would not play again until the 2001 GMAC Bowl in Mobile. The city of Mobile is the original U.S. home for Mardi Gras. The Pirates had played TCU in the inaugural Mobile Bowl in 1999, and this was the third year in a row with a bowl invitation. The bowl committee did a nice job with a parade and events surrounding the game, which is played at Ladd-Peebles stadium, the longtime home of the Senior Bowl. There was much anticipation among Pirate fans about going back to Mobile and playing Marshall.

For most East Carolina fans, the 2001 GMAC Bowl was simply a nightmare. It's hard to describe it any other way. The game pitted two future NFL quarterbacks against each other, David Garrard for ECU and Byron Leftwich for Marshall. Garrard and Leftwich would later be NFL teammates on the Jacksonville Jaguars.

The game started out all ECU. Three turnovers by Marshall and a potent offense made it 38-8 at the half, and several thousand fans left at halftime. The second half was mostly Marshall, though, as David Garrard threw two interceptions that were returned for touchdowns. Marshall got the ball back, trailing by 6, on their own 20 with only 50 seconds remaining and no timeouts. Leftwich threw the tying touchdown with only seven seconds remaining, making the score 51-51. They only needed the extra point to win, but they missed!

The agony continued as the game moved to overtime. Both

teams traded touchdowns in the first OT while Marshall held the Pirates to a field goal in the second overtime. Leftwich connected on the winning pass and the final score was 64-61. The game is still the second biggest comeback in FBS bowl history and the highest total score in bowl history.

Marshall moved from the MAC to Conference USA in 2005, setting up an annual clash with the Pirates. The first game was in Huntington and it was the first time ECU had played there in 36 years. We made the trip and the Pirates won a close game 34-29, but the most remarkable part of the experience was meeting the Marshall fans.

For Marshall fans, the 1970 plane crash was a defining moment, not only for the university and the football program, but also for the city of Huntington and the region. They have a memorial fountain on campus that is turned off every year on November 14th, the anniversary of the crash. It is turned back on each year on the first day of spring. Because the opponent was East Carolina and the plane was returning from that game, Marshall fans instantly recognized Pirates and shared their stories. The two schools are linked forever by that tragedy.

On that trip in 2005, literally dozens of people welcomed us to Huntington. Before the game, the Marshall cheerleaders came into the ECU visitor section and welcomed us to campus. At dinner after the game at the Marshall Hall of Fame Café, people noticed our ECU shirts and came up and welcomed us to town. Usually, the home fans welcome visitors with their middle finger. That had been our experience elsewhere in West Virginia. The most poignant moment came as we were leaving town the next morning. We stopped at a Starbucks for a coffee to go. The young lady behind the counter noticed our Pirate shirts and asked if we had been to yesterday's game. We of course said "yes". She told us that her dad had been a student at Marshall and was working for the campus newspaper in 1970.

She said, "He has never gotten over it." The expression "It's more than a game," is certainly true for Marshall University football.

On our way back to North Carolina, I mentioned to my wife that I had heard rumors for years that there was a plaque or memorial to the 1970 Marshall team at Dowdy Ficklen Stadium, but I had never seen it. After I returned, I called ECU AD Terry Holland and asked him what he knew about it. He said that as far as he knew there was nothing at ECU memorializing the lives lost in the crash. I suggested that maybe we should do something and unveil it in November of 2006 when Marshall played in Greenville for the first time since 1978. That game would fall three days before the anniversary of the plane crash. He said that he thought it was a great idea. Over the next year, our athletic department came up with a design that was approved by Marshall. The focal point of the memorial shows the fountain from the Marshall campus. The plaque was installed on the northeast corner of the stadium outside the gate near the visitors locker room. It was unveiled by the Marshall president and the ECU chancellor in a ceremony prior to the 2006 game, and today it is a visible reminder of the special bond between our schools.

The nine games between ECU and Marshall from 2005 to 2013 as members of Conference USA were split 6-3, with ECU winning six. Like the GMAC Bowl, three of those games ended in overtime. The 2013 game was the most disappointing. The winner of the game would play for the Conference USA championship. The Pirates were heavily favored, having only lost two games by a combined score of eight points. ECU lost 59-28 in a game that was never close.

Most recently, the 2020 game scheduled for Greenville was canceled due to Covid. It was a shame because it was the fiftieth anniversary year of the plane crash and set for a large national stage as the season opener. The 2021 game went on as scheduled. A large group of former players from ECU went to Huntington for the game and paid their respects at the cemetery where most of the victims of the crash are buried. The game was special for the Pirates, who came from behind in the last 7:31 to score three touchdowns and win the game 42-38. This game really turned the season around for the Pirates and was the first of seven wins in 2021.

Marshall University struggles in the shadow of West Virginia University. While WVU is in Morgantown, a true college town, Marshall is in Huntington. It sits on the Ohio River and has benefited from the river location, but the city has lost manufacturing jobs and lost population. The city has slightly more than half as many people as it did sixty years ago. The university is vital to the city.

My Marshall Travel Log:

Visited the campus memorial to the 1970 plane crash victims

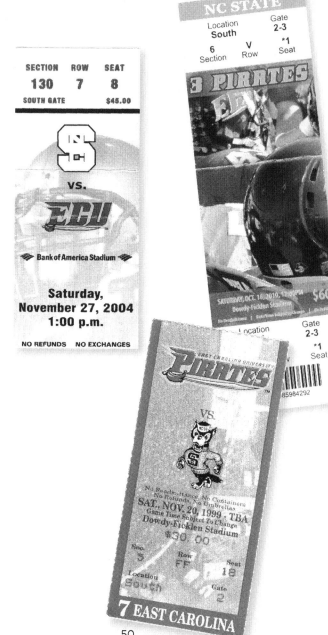

SATURDAY
September 10, 2016
DOWDY-FICKLEN STADIUM
Remittance   Date Subject to Change   No Refunds

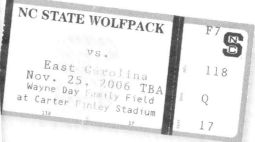

North Carolina State University (NCSU)

North Carolina State fans would say that this series is not a rivalry. While I may be wearing my purple glasses again, most objective people would view it differently. The series started in 1970, and for the next half century the teams have played thirty-two times. It began with the first eighteen games all played in Raleigh and played in consecutive years from 1970 until the infamous 1987 game.

The eighteen games in Raleigh were largely NC State-dominated, with the Wolfpack winning twelve of those first eighteen games at home. My first experience with the Wolfpack came in 1973 when I traveled to see the Pirates lose 57-8. This was the second year of the Lou Holtz era; Holtz won all four times that his Wolfpack team played the Pirates. He would not lose a game to ECU until 1999, in his first home game at South Carolina.

The ECU and NCSU series was abruptly paused after the game in Raleigh in 1987. After that 32-14 Pirate victory, fans came down the grassy hill in the south endzone, tore down the chain link fence, and swarmed that endzone. They were met by security and some State fans. There were many conflicting reports about exactly what happened, with most of the differences depending on whether your favorite color was purple or red. A large fight ensued, and the long-term result was the cancellation of the series by NC State Athletic Director Jim Valvano.

Both the Pirates and State coach Dick Sheridan wanted to resume the series. The NCSU administration ruled against it, but the 1992 Peach Bowl brought the teams together for one of the most memorable games in ECU history. In the last almost-thirty years, it appears that I may be the only Pirate fan to not attend the Peach Bowl. I had tickets to the game, but my wife had the flu and was barely able to get out of bed. She told me to go ahead and head for Atlanta, but I chose to stay in Raleigh. It was probably the best choice! Much has been written by others about the 1992 Peach Bowl. I have spoken with players, coaches and fans who were at the game. I will let those comments stand. It was a magical moment.

The next thirteen games from 1996 to 2022 were evenly split between Greenville and Raleigh, with two at a neutral site in Charlotte. There were some very exciting games during those years. One overlooked fact is that in four of those years, the ECU versus NC State game was the final game for four different head coaches. Two ECU coaches and two State coaches suffered a final defeat against their rival.

With the threatened intervention of the North Carolina General Assembly, the series resumed in Charlotte in 1996. The much-anticipated resumption of the series drew what was then the largest crowd to ever see a college football game in North Carolina. The Pirate fans in attendance were not disappointed on that chilly damp Saturday after Thanksgiving. The Pirates held the Pack on their first possession, and on the third ECU offensive play of the game Scott Harley broke through the line and headed 75 yards straight for the endzone. From my seat near the 10-yard line, he appeared to break out of the low fog on the field and come straight toward me. It was almost like the players coming out of the purple fog during the team entrance at Dowdy-Ficklen. Later he had another touchdown run of more than 50 yards.

Harley finished the game with 351 yards, which is still the ECU single-game rushing record. It also unfortunately turned out to be the last Pirate game of the season, since despite an 8-3 record they did not get a bowl invitation. Harley's total of 1,745 yards for the season in eleven games is also still an ECU record. The Pirate fans rolled out of Charlotte that night with a record-breaking crowd, a record-breaking rushing performance and a 50-29 win. Nothing runs like a Harley.

The next game was the following year in Raleigh. It was the first game in the series in Raleigh since the fighting in 1987. ECU and State both came into the game with 5-5 records. The first half was all defense, with the Pirates leading 3-0 at halftime. It was 24-24 all with 3:39 left in the game when the Pack went on an 82-yard, 9-play drive to take the lead. With 30 seconds left, ECU quarterback Danny Gonzalez's pass was picked off and returned for a touchdown to make the final score 37-24. Both teams came into the game hoping for a bowl bid, but there was none. In a game that State fans said was not a rivalry and meant nothing to them, celebrating Wolfpack fans tore down the goalposts.

Up next, in 1999, was possibly the most anticipated game in Dowdy-Ficklen Stadium history. It was the first-ever visit to Greenville by NC State. After almost thirty years and twenty-one games, the Wolfpack was finally heading east. This was before the endzone Boneyard seating was added. The stadium capacity was 43,000 and bleachers were added to the endzones. 50,000 fans made it inside the stadium that day. This was the largest crowd to that point in the history of the stadium and the first time with attendance of more than 50,000 people. Not only did the crowd anticipate playing the Wolfpack in Greenville, but also the Pirates were ranked No. 21 in the country and were having a magical season after wins over Miami, South Carolina, Duke, and West Virginia. The game was even in terms of yardage, and both teams put together good drives. The Pirates were unlucky when David Garrard fumbled going into the endzone, and the Pack was unlucky when in the red zone, they had three back-to-back penalties to kill the drive. While the yardage was even, the Pirates were much more efficient in scoring. The final score was 23-6 Pirates. ECU received an invitation on the field immediately following the game to play in the inaugural GMAC Bowl in Mobile. The next morning, NC State coach Mike O'Cain was fired and became the first of four coaches to end their tenure after a game in this rivalry.

The next coach to lose his job in the rivalry would be ECU's John Thompson. The next game in the series was five years later in 2004 and it was once again played in Charlotte. Neither team was having a good year. The Pirates had only won two games and the Wolfpack had only won four. Neither team was going to a bowl no matter the outcome of this game. That was a considerable contrast to the game in Charlotte eight years earlier which had 20,000 more fans and was the renewal of the rivalry. ECU tried a new look with egg-yolk-yellow jerseys, and the ugly jerseys matched the ugly play on the field. The Pirates looked inept. They only gained 140 yards of total offense. After bumbling through four quarters, the final score was 52-14 State. John Thompson had officially resigned ten days earlier, and he walked off the field that day for the last time as a Pirate.

Heading to Raleigh in 2006, the Pirates were 6-5 with an up-and down season under Skip Holtz. Holtz knew much about the Wolfpack from his father's days in Raleigh when he was a child. The game was typical of the Holtz era with a strong defensive effort and just enough big plays to win the game. A 53-yard pass from James Pinkney to Aundrae Allison with only four seconds remaining in the first half put the Pirates ahead for good. The final score was 21-16 in favor of ECU. With just a few seconds remaining on the game clock, NC State officials stopped the clock and lowered the goalposts to avoid any possible celebration by East Carolina fans. A few moments later, coach Chuck Amato walked slowly past the lowered goal posts and off the field at Carter-Finley Stadium for the last time.

The series came to Greenville in 2007, and the Pirates just didn't have a good day. Chris Johnson had a touchdown but the defense gave up three first-half touchdowns. The Wolfpack hung on to win 34-20. But things were different in 2008 when the Pirates traveled to Raleigh, ranked No. 15 and No. 16 in the polls after beating ranked Virginia Tech and West Virginia teams. The previous week the Pirates had barely defeated Tulane in New Orleans, but it came at a big price. Senior linebacker Quinton Cotton was lost for the year. Cotton was one of the stars on Greg Hudson's defense and would be really missed the remainder of the year. Stanley Bryant, the left tackle on the blindside, was injured as well and also out for the season.

The game against NC State was tight, but the Pirates were mostly in control near the end. This was Russell Wilson's first home start and he led the Wolfpack down the field and threw the tying touchdown with just over a minute to play. It was his third touchdown of the game. It went to overtime, and State would score first. When the Pirates got the ball, Patrick Pinkney dropped back to pass. A State defensive lineman hurdled the freshman left tackle who had replaced Bryant and hit Pinkney in the back, causing a fumble that NC State recovered. It's hard to replace a senior offensive lineman with a freshman, especially at left tackle, and in this case it was costly. The ranked and favored Pirates lost 30-24, commencing a three-game slide.

The next meeting also featured Russell Wilson and overtime, but it was a much different game. We all have our favorite players and our favorite teams and our favorite games. The 2010 ECU versus NC State game in Greenville was one of my favorites. With over 50,000 fans in attendance, it was simply a great game. Dominique Davis hit his first 14 passes in a row and ran for one yard on what would be the winning score. He never turned the ball over. Russell Wilson was intercepted three times. In the fourth quarter, the Wolfpack kicked a field goal with less than three minutes to play to take a three-point lead. The Pirates answered a minute later with a field goal of their own to tie the game. In overtime, State won the toss and elected to start on defense. The Pirates chose the direction of play and selected the east end, The Boneyard end. Davis ran for one yard and a score, but Michael Barbour missed the extra point, giving ECU only a six-point lead. State ran the ball to the 17-yard line and then Russell Wilson attempted a pass to the goal line. He never saw freshman safety Damon Magazu crossing just in front of the receiver. Magazu made a great catch and went to the ground to secure the Pirate win. Russell Wilson was 1-1 against the Pirates in two games, both in overtime and ending on defensive plays. No goalposts were harmed that day.

The teams did not play for three years until the Pirates made the trip to Raleigh in 2013. ECU was on a roll late in the season at 8-2. It was Dave Doeren's first year, and the Wolfpack was struggling. People say that imitation is the sincerest form of flattery, so East Carolina should have been flattered when social media showed that NC State had used the Pirate-state-of-mind type logo, putting the wolf head in the middle of their field. They quickly covered it up, but on game day the outline of the state of N.C. was very plain behind the State block "S." Also, the State fans were restless because they had fired a somewhat popular coach and now had an unknown quantity and a losing season. The Pirates led by Shane Carden were dominant. They had a 35-7 lead going into the fourth quarter and a 42-14 lead with a minute to play in the game. Only two quick State touchdowns made the score a more respectable 42-28. Long before that final minute, the State fans had found the exits. State had tried a new seating strategy, putting opposing fans in the upper decks in the four corners of the stadium. This worked well for the thousands of ECU fans in attendance, as we did the "Purple-Gold" cheer across the field at each other! Some games are just fun. This one was fun.

Again it was three years before the teams met again in Greenville in 2016. This time the Pirates had a new coach. It was Scottie Montgomery's second game after blasting Western Carolina 52-7 the previous week. The State team would finish a pretty good season at 7-6 with a bowl win and a win at home over Notre Dame. The hot noon game was a sellout, with more than 50,000 in the stadium. It was the second-largest crowd in Dowdy-Ficklen history. Starting for State was Ryan Finley, a junior transfer from Boise State. The Pirates went with transfer senior Phillip Nelson and later James Summers in the wildcat. The game had six lead changes, but the one that counted near the end belonged to ECU. Anthony Scott scored from five yards out with six minutes to play, and the Pirates held on to win. Dave Doeren's future looked uncertain; Scottie Montgomery's future looked bright.

The next two games were forgettable at best. In 2018, Hurricane Florence caused the Pirates to not travel to Blacksburg and play Virginia Tech, and the Wolfpack had to cancel a game with West Virginia, so a game was scheduled on December 1 in Raleigh. The Pirates were outplayed and completely embarrassed 58-6. While David Blackwell was officially the ECU coach that afternoon in Raleigh since Scottie Montgomery had been fired two days earlier, Scottie was really the second ECU coach to end his career with the Wolfpack.

Since the 2018 game was the last game of the year, the 2019 game was nine months later and the first game of the year. The game in Raleigh was a sellout. This again challenges the notion that this is not a rivalry. Coach Mike Houston's team was short on speed and was not physical enough and lost control of the game after the first drive. The final score on a hot Saturday was 34-6. With only two field goals, the Pirates never crossed the goal line.

The 2022 game was more than a sellout; it set the attendance record for Dowdy-Ficklen Stadium. The previous record was set in 2014 against North Carolina. 51,711 fans saw a great football game. There was as much hype and anticipation as any game played in Greenville. With an ESPN telecast and a noon start, it had all the makings of a major game. The fans saw a game with ups and downs and outstanding defensive play by the Pirates. With two goal-line stands against the Wolfpack late in the game, one of those generating a turnover at the one-yard line, NC State did not score at all in the second half. State did major damage by blocking and recovering a punt in the endzone. In the end, the Pirates would score to potentially tie the game but miss the extra point. The defense held and gave the offense one more opportunity, but a 41-yard game winning field goal missed the mark, stunning the huge crowd. The heavily favored and No. 13-ranked Wolfpack escaped Greenville with a 21-20 win.

While NC State dominated the first eighteen years of games played in Raleigh, the last fourteen games split between home and home and neutral sites are dead even at seven wins for each team. For fifty years these teams have played some great games. The facts are clear; this is the definition of a rivalry.

West Virginia University (WVU)

West Virginia and East Carolina share a forty-seven-year history in football. It began in 1970 and ended most recently in 2017. A future game in Greenville is scheduled for 2026. In discussing WVU and ECU there are two notable things. First there is the West Virginia football culture. This has changed radically in the last twenty-five years. Second, while the two schools have played twenty-two times, the Pirates have won only three games. In the nineteen losses, thirteen have been decided by three or more scores.

WVU and East Carolina share a number of similarities. Both are large public universities with similar enrollments. Both schools have medicine, nursing and dentistry. The schools are relatively isolated from other parts of the state and are essentially rural. The all-important television markets are very small. Both are true college towns that are almost within the shadow of a much-larger city, Raleigh and Pittsburgh.

The Pirates have had a few close losses to WVU, but the most painful one came in 1996. The Mountaineers contained ECU quarterback Marcus Crandell most of the game. ECU slightly outgained WVU but simply could not find the endzone. Late in the fourth quarter, Crandell led the Pirates on a 67-yard drive in

57 seconds to make the score 10-9 in favor of WVU. With only 10 seconds remaining, Coach Steve Logan sent Crandell to try for the two-point conversion. The pass was incomplete and West Virginia won the game 10-9. Logan took a lot of heat for that decision. This prompted the famous Steve Logan line, "When you are at East Carolina, you go for it every time or you don't coach at East Carolina." Incidentally, 1996 was the first year of the then-new overtime rules in D-1 college football. ECU would not play its first overtime game until five years later.

The fan culture is similar, but West Virginia has been more extreme, in some ways like the SEC. By 2000, most ECU fans who traveled to games in Morgantown would consider the atmosphere there out-of-control. Walking up to the stadium for visiting fans was a bad experience. You would be cursed, and often the WVU fans would throw beer cans at you. You would have to pass "The Pit," which is a student tailgating area surrounded by a chain link fence. For a 6 p.m. home game, The Pit would open at 8 a.m. and be filled with pickup trucks, many of which had beer kegs in the back. The alcohol-fueled students did their best to intimidate the visitors.

Hundreds of coeds would wear navy T-shirts with the school logo modified to say "West F&cking Virginia". The fans in the stands were known to throw batteries at the visiting sidelines. At one game in Morgantown in the early 2000s, a 75-year old woman, an ECU fan, was hit in the head by a bottle thrown by a young WVU fan. The lady was bleeding and had to be escorted out for medical attention. Even the nearby WVU fans identified the young man who threw the bottle, but security did nothing at all. I wrote a letter to then WVU President Hardesty about the fan behavior issue. I received a reply from an assistant basically saying that fan behavior is a problem everywhere. They did not acknowledge the bad fan behavior or address the situation in Morgantown.

It appears that two things changed this culture at West Virginia. The entrance into the Big 12 in 2012 meant that visiting fans from schools like Texas, Oklahoma and Texas Tech were less tolerant of this behavior from the newest member of the conference. The second factor was a new academic administration. At a joint Pirate Club/ECU Alumni Association event in Morgantown in 2017, there were two WVU ambassadors stationed at the door. These were two retired professors who welcomed the ECU fans and mingled with the crowd. The next day walking into the stadium, I was greeted by dozens of West Virginia fans who said, "Welcome to Morgantown," and similar things. It was a huge change from the six previous trips I had made to WVU. The change in administration was a major influence as well. Dr. Gordon Gee became the president of West Virginia University in 2013 shortly after its move to the Big 12. He had been the president at Ohio State and Vanderbilt prior to coming to Morgantown. There had been controversy at both schools, but he had a good grip on athletics after many years in the SEC and the Big 10. I emailed Dr. Gee and told him my observations about the radical change in Morgantown. It was clear in my correspondence with him after the game that he understood college athletics and relationships. He thanked me for my comments and seemed pleased that things had changed at WVU.

After eight games, finally in 1995 the Pirates were able to beat the Mountaineers. It wasn't easy. While the Pirate offense moved the ball effectively through the air in the first half to take a 20-9 lead, the second half was a different story. West Virginia would score 11 unanswered points to tie the game, and then the Pirates answered with a field goal to lead 23-20. An ECU fumble with 44 seconds remaining in the game gave the Mountaineers some hope, but the Pirate defense held on. It was ECU's first victory in the series, and the Pirates would finish the season 9-3.

The one and only neutral site game between these teams occurred to open the 1999 season. While Hurricane Dennis was making landfall east of Greenville at Cape Lookout, the Pirates and Mountaineers were preparing to play at Bank of America Stadium in Charlotte under partly cloudy skies and temperatures in the 80s. ECU Athletic Director Mike Hamrick joked that he had known that a hurricane was going to hit the coast and that's why the game was scheduled in Charlotte. While the Pirates were led by future NFL quarterback David Garrard, the Mountaineers had their own future NFL quarterback with Mark Bulger. Even with two future NFL quarterbacks it was the ground game, especially for the Pirates, that made the difference. ECU had 327 rushing yards split between running back Jamie Wilson and Garrard. A 1-yard sneak by David Garrard with only 56 seconds left in the game gave the Pirates the lead and the game. In front of almost 50,000 fans, the final score would be 30-23.

In many ways, the most significant win in the series was in 2008. The Pirates had just defeated No. 17 Virginia Tech the previous week and the Mountaineers came into Dowdy-Ficklen stadium ranked No. 8 in the country. The Pirate offense controlled the game, and quarterback Patrick Pinkney went 22-28 and put together multiple long drives. He engineered four drives with more than 10 plays each, and three resulted in touchdowns. While the offense controlled the clock, it was the defense, especially the defensive line, that won the day. The defensive line was anchored by C.J. Wilson, Linval Joseph and Jay Ross, all future NFL players. For the entire game, West Virginia only got inside the ECU 30-yard line once, resulting in the field goal that would be their only score of the game. The Pirates had been underdogs but simply dominated the game 24-3. The Mountaineers would finish the season 9-4 and ranked No.23. Their other three losses were by a combined 10 points.

It was a complete defensive victory for Skip Holtz and his team against a well-coached and talented West Virginia team.

University of North Carolina (UNC)

The history here is clear but also clouded by emotions. Many Pirate fans consider North Carolina State as ECU's biggest rival, but I would argue that "the school in Chapel Hill" is a much bigger rival.

A rivalry is a competitive relationship, and this rivalry started before these teams ever played a single down on the football field. In 1964, when the idea was first floated to build a medical school in Greenville, it drew immediate opposition from the administration in Chapel Hill. In 1965, when Dr. Leo Jenkins proposed university status for East Carolina College, it met with similar opposition. The reason, although not openly stated, was that the UNC supporters feared a loss of resources. They believed that any funds to create and operate a medical school or establish a university would come from their budget. At the time, the East Carolina budget was a separate item within the state budget and not tied to the UNC System budget. It was thought to be a zero-sum game.

ECU and Dr. Jenkins won the university status battle with the inclusion of several other state-supported schools. He built a coalition of supporters of those schools and their members of the North Carolina General Assembly. Many believed that Dr.

Jenkins would not accept university status if it meant being on par with some of the HBCUs, but he proved them wrong.

The medical school fight proved much more difficult. Many have said that the creation of a medical school at East Carolina University was the single most contentious issue of the 1970s within the North Carolina General Assembly. Dr. Jenkins put together a strong legislative group to support the medical school. At that time, legislators in eastern North Carolina were a powerful group. It only took a small group of legislators from outside the region to join in and create a majority. Many legislators from the piedmont and mountains who came from rural areas joined with the folks from the east. After more than ten years Leo Jenkins, with the help of many influential politicians, got the vote he wanted. Dean Christopher Fordham of the UNC medical school called this "a potential educational tragedy." Fordham later became the chancellor at UNC. When UNC President William Friday saw that this was inevitable, he quickly changed sides and became a supporter of the ECU medical school. Years later he stated that he originally opposed the medical school because he didn't believe that the state could afford a second medical school. The real reason appeared to be that his supporters were against the idea.

There are a lot of ECU folks who don't realize the hard feelings that were created in the '70s from this fight. It was statewide, and the lines were clearly drawn. There isn't space to name all of those who were responsible for getting the medical school approved. Lots of people have taken credit over the last fifty years, but without the determination and leadership of Leo Jenkins, it would not have become a reality. But don't think it stopped when the doors to the Brody School of Medicine opened in 1977. There was also a lot of pushback on the creation of the East Carolina Heart Institute. Later, more than thirty years after the fight for the medical school ended, we were again in the midst of an effort to prevent the creation of the ECU School of Dental Medicine. The same tired arguments from the '70s were brought out again. This was primarily led by the NC Dental Society who made significant political contributions to the members of the NC General Assembly. Their push was to add students to the UNC dental school instead of building a new dental school at ECU. In the end, the idea of building dental learning centers in rural and underserved areas prevailed. The general assembly funded both the new dental school in Greenville and the expansion of the existing dental school in Chapel Hill. More hard feelings were created for a second time.

Athletic director Clarence Stasavich had the difficult task of trying to get the administration in Chapel Hill to schedule a football series with the Pirates in the '70s with the medical school fight in the background. Stasavich was successful, and the first game was played in Chapel Hill in 1972. The series was played annually through 1981 with the exception of two years, 1974 and 1977. Of course all the games were played in Chapel Hill.

The first game was a UNC rout, but the second game was surprisingly close. The Tar Heels won a very close game in 1973 by a score of 28-27. Then in 1975, the football rivalry between ECU and UNC would be changed forever. On Friday, October 24, 1975, athletic director and former coach Clarence Stasavich suddenly passed away. There was talk about canceling the game scheduled for the next day, but Stasavich's widow insisted that the Pirates play the game in memory of Stas. Coach Pat Dye's Pirates made the trip to Chapel Hill and after the first UNC score, it was all ECU. In ECU's own "win one for the Gipper" story, the Pirates dominated and won easily 38-17. The memory of Stas was ECU's 12th man that October day in Chapel Hill. Considering the opponent and the circumstances, most would agree that this was the most significant victory in the then-43-

year history of ECU football. The program built by Coach Stas and fine-tuned by Pat Dye had turned the corner.

It was hard to top the 1975 game, but the next two games were very close UNC wins, 12-10 and 14-10. In the 12-10 loss, ECU was the only team to score a touchdown while the Heels kicked four field goals. The 1979 game ended in a 24-24 tie. The two teams would play twice more in 1980 and 1981, both times with UNC winning big. That was the end of the series as far as UNC was concerned.

Six years after the last game in Chapel Hill, NC State canceled their series with the Pirates. This came after the famous "riot" at Carter Finley Stadium in 1987. ECU folks wanted to play these games, but with the success the Pirates had achieved, they wanted only a home-and-home series with each school. No longer would ECU make the trip to Raleigh or Chapel Hill without a return trip. The Pirates had made twenty-six road trips to the Triangle. The argument from both UNC and NC State was that they had "nothing to gain."

In 1995 Senator Ed Warren of Pitt County filed Senate Bill 607, entitled "An Act to Require the University of North Carolina and North Carolina State University to Play East Carolina University in Football." It's important to note that the bill had some supporters outside of eastern North Carolina and it had twenty-three co-sponsors. This meant that Senator Warren and the other sponsors only needed three more votes to get this passed into law. He outlined the economic impact of in-state schools playing each other and the "fairness" to taxpayers across the state. Why should UNC and NC State schedule games with out-of-state schools when they could play East Carolina and all the money would remain here in North Carolina? There was an implied threat to their funding.

This was a serious blow to UNC and NCSU and their supporters. Eventually after much bickering, Senator Warren withdrew the bill, but only after all three schools had agreed to play each other and started working on a schedule. The NCSU series started again in 1996, while the UNC series resumed in 2001.

The highly anticipated game in 2001 came just three weeks after 9/11. There was a lot of tension unrelated to football. Of course the series had to restart in Chapel Hill, but there were games set the next two years in Greenville. Tickets for ECU fans were hard to find, but some desperate folks even bought a UNC season ticket package and sold the other tickets, just to get into that game.

It was a game of what should have been for the Pirates. ECU controlled the game in the first quarter and led 10-0. The Pirates were driving near the UNC 30 when David Garrard attempted to hit an open receiver in the endzone. The ball was batted at the line of scrimmage and intercepted, ending the drive. The game-winning touchdown for the Tar Heels came on a pass through the arms of an ECU defender to a UNC player who had fallen and was lying on the ground in the endzone. The most disappointing play was a spectacular 76-yard kickoff return by ECU's Art Brown in the third quarter. The ball was punched out just before Brown crossed the goal line, bouncing harmlessly out of the endzone for a touchback. Three big plays determined the outcome. None went ECU's way.

The next meeting between the ECU and UNC would be in 2003 and would be the Tar Heels' first-ever trip to Greenville. For more than thirty years, the road had only gone toward the west. Unfortunately for the Pirates, this was arguably ECU's worst team since the 1950s, or maybe even the 1930s. While UNC would finish the year 2-10, the Pirates would lose the game 28-17 and finish the season 1-11 in John Thompson's first season.

It would be four years before the next meeting. That game was in Greenville for only the second time. By 2007, Skip Holtz was well on his way to turning the program around. The teams were evenly matched and the score was tied at 17 at the half and 31 at the end of the third quarter. Patrick Pinkney had over 400 yards passing, 136 of which were thrown to Chris Johnson who only had 18 yards rushing. The game ended as time expired and Ben Hartman kicked a 39-yard field goal. Hartman had missed three of four attempts from inside 40 yards earlier in the game. Hartman was mobbed by his teammates. It was ECU's first win over the Tar Heels since 1975 and their first win in Greenville. The Pirates gave new coach Butch Davis his first loss at UNC.

The teams did not play in 2008, but in 2009 Skip Holtz took the Pirates to Chapel Hill hoping to repeat the success of 2007 in Greenville. The Tar Heels won the game, but had to vacate the victory due to the scandal of players receiving improper benefits from agents. A total of sixteen wins were vacated in 2008 and 2009.

The next three ECU-versus-UNC games were under ECU coach Ruffin McNeill. Ruff's teams lost by large margins all three times in 2010, 2011 and 2012. That all changed in 2013.

After a disappointing loss to Virginia Tech 10-15 during the previous week, the Pirates traveled to Chapel Hill once more looking for their second-ever win at Kenan Stadium. Their last win in Chapel Hill had been in 1975, thirty-eight years earlier. They were 12-1/2 point underdogs that day. ECU dominated this game with more than 600 yards of offense, including 196 rushing yards by Vintavious Cooper. The final score was 55-31 in a stadium that at the end only had purple-clad fans. Shane Carden had a great day with almost 400 yards passing and he even conducted the ECU Marching Pirates when they played the fight song after the game. Most Pirates who were there that day had their best day and the most fun ever in Chapel Hill. Many of us stayed to savor the moment. One overserved ECU student said to me as I was leaving the stadium, "I don't want to ever leave."

Thanks to UNC, the game in 2014 made for one of the best days ever in Greenville. The Tar Heels came to Greenville ranked No. 25. The Pirates had started the season with wins over NC Central and Virginia Tech and a loss at South Carolina. It was ECU's first season in the American Athletic Conference since leaving Conference USA after seventeen seasons.

The game started with the Pirates scoring first, but by early in the second quarter UNC held a 20-14 lead. The Pirates scored three more touchdowns in the second period and led 35-20 at halftime. The turning point of the game came in the first minute of the second half, when Pirate linebacker Zeek Bigger intercepted a pass and took it 46 yards for a score. From that moment forward, the end result was never in doubt. Bigger also had 17 tackles in the game. The Pirates just could not be stopped. At the end, the Pirates had rolled up 789 total yards of offense. It was a school record. It was also a record-setting day for the Tar Heels. The 70 points, 789 yards, and 39 first downs given up by their defense were all records. With two minutes remaining in the game, the chant was "Our State" from most of the 51,082 fans in purple. It may be a cliché, but it was a great day to be a Pirate and 70-41 will be remembered for a long time in the history of ECU football. No one who was there that day will ever forget the cannon firing over and over again.

The final scheduled game of the series was played four years later in Greenville in 2018. This was Scottie Montgomery's third year, and things had not gone like most Pirate fans had hoped. He only had six wins in two seasons, and only a win against NC State was truly meaningful. Coming off a surprising loss at home to North Carolina A&T, ECU was determined to prove that 55-31 in 2013 and 70-41 in 2014 were not flukes. While the first half was close, the Pirates took a 21-19 lead into the dressing room. The second half was dominated by the ECU defense that did not give up a score. The Pirates didn't get almost 800 yards of offense like in 2014, but 500 yards and great defense was more than enough. The final score was 41-19. Unfortunately, there were no more games scheduled and there is nothing like Senate Bill 607 in the works. There should be more games in this series. The only consolation that the Pirates have is that in the last three games with UNC, they have scored 166 points and won all three games convincingly. The sound of the cannon from that day in 2014 still rings in Pirate ears.

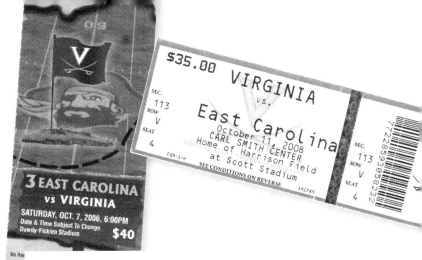

The University of Virginia (UVA)

Both schools would agree that the University of Virginia is definitely not an ECU rival. While both schools have long football histories, we have only played three times. This may seem surprising since the two schools are only three-and-a-half hours apart in neighboring states.

UVA began playing football in the 1880s, and their only real rival over these years has been Virginia Tech. While they may consider UNC or another ACC team a rival, this is really a one-sided rivalry. Since 1915, the only coach with any real success was George Welch, who came to UVA from Navy where he had played in the 1950s. During his eighteen years at Virginia, he won slightly more than sixty percent of his games and two ACC championships.

Welch was succeeded by Al Groh. He had played at Virginia and had a long history in both the NFL and in college football. Groh had coached for five different NFL teams following five not-very-productive years at Wake Forest. He was hired by Athletic Director Terry Holland in 2000 and he coached at UVA for the next nine years.

When Terry Holland became the AD at East Carolina, he began an aggressive scheduling campaign. That included two games with the University of Virginia, among other ACC schools. The games were scheduled for 2006 and 2008.

Virginia's first trip to Greenville was in 2006 with an Al Groh team versus a Skip Holtz team. It was simply a solid performance for the Pirates. They led the entire game, dominating the statistics and the time of possession and winning the game 31-21. Groh said that they were out coached and that the Pirates were very physical. The Cavaliers would finish the season with a 5-7 record.

The return game came two years later in 2008, but unfortunately with a different outcome. The Pirates had the early advantage with two interceptions, but they had to settle for two Ben Hartman field goals. The ECU defense could not stop the UVA running game. The Pirates staged a late comeback, but it would not be enough. The Cavaliers would win the game 35-20, and like in 2006 finish the season at 5-7.

The most interesting game for many Pirate fans was the only other game in this series. It happened in 1975. In many ways, this game was more about the coaches than the teams. Virginia was coached by Sonny Randle, who had come there directly from ECU. He had great success with the Pirates and had won back-to-back Southern Conference championships in 1972 and 1973. At the end of the 1973 season, Randle was given a car by the grateful Pirate fans, but he promptly left for Virginia where he had played college football before a very good ten-year NFL career as a wide receiver. Fans at the time said, "We gave him a new car to drive to Virginia." The popular coach was no longer a fan favorite in Greenville.

The Pirates traveled to Charlottesville with revenge on their minds. This was just two weeks after the Pirates' first-ever win in Chapel Hill. Coach Pat Dye was no stranger to these types of games, and he would show no mercy on Virginia or Sonny Randle. Most of the Pirate players had been recruited by Randle. There were mixed feelings among the players about Sonny Randle, but they definitely wanted to win the game and they did. The Pirates ran up and down the field at will. Virginia got a late touchdown, but the final score told the real story—61-10. The Pirates had 690 total yards of offense, which at the time was a record. They ran for 642 yards and 9 touchdowns. Both of those records still stand almost fifty years later. The margin of victory was the third most in ECU history, another record still standing after ninety years of football.

When Sonny Randle left East Carolina after just three seasons in 1973, he stated that the difference between ECU and Virginia was "apples and oranges." After the game, ECU fans threw apples and oranges at Randle. In two weeks, Virginia would finish a 1-10 year and Sonny Randle would be gone after two losing seasons at his alma mater. He coached two seasons at a prep school and finished his coaching career after five very disappointing seasons at Marshall. Sonny Randle was elected to the ECU Athletics Hall of Fame. While the ECU versus Virginia story is a short one, it included a large serving of revenge—not for the school, but the coach.

Duke University

Since the 1960s, Duke has been the perfect example of a basketball school. While they did host the Rose Bowl in 1942 when the attack on Pearl Harbor prompted organizers to move it off the West Coast, football has been an afterthought since those days. While other similar schools were investing in football facilities, Duke really didn't invest until 2015 and later. The lack of investment in facilities really was a sign of the lack of interest in the football program. In the crowded Triangle media market, Duke football was just not very important. Only six winning seasons in the past twenty-two years is the result of the lack of real interest in football at Duke.

East Carolina and Duke share some history. Mike McGee, a Duke alumnus, coached the Pirates for only one season in 1970. He went a mediocre 3-8 and returned to his alma mater the following year. He remained there for seven years, but never with much success. In his two best years, he was only 6-5. The Pirates also shared Scottie Montgomery with Duke. Montgomery spent three years at his alma mater under David Cutcliffe before coming to ECU in 2016. Montgomery's years at Duke were some of the best years of Cutcliff's tenure, including a ten-win season in 2013.

The Pirates played Duke twice in the '70s, twice in the '80s, three times in the '90s and three times in the 2000s. The two schools have split the ten meetings. Only two games were played in Greenville, with the Pirates winning both.

The Blue Devils' first trip to Greenville came in 1999 and was a 27-9 win for the Pirates. It was coach Carl Franks' first season. It was the second game of a five-game winning streak to start the season for ECU. The Pirates were the better and more physical team. Duke finished the season 3-8.

The following season, ECU opened with Duke in Durham. Duke did not put up much of a fight. From the beginning it was clear that ECU would win and they did, 38-0. Duke would go winless that year, 0-11.

In 2002, both teams opened their seasons in Durham. The game was played in a driving rainstorm. This didn't help the ECU passing game where new starting quarterback Paul Troth threw three interceptions, one of which was returned for a touchdown. This was the first game with someone other than David Garrard starting in almost four years. On the first play of the game, Troth fumbled the snap and Duke recovered. The Pirates gave up twenty unanswered points by the middle of the second quarter and never were able to rally. With only 25 rushing yards and awful passing conditions, the Pirates never got the momentum and lost 23-16. The Blue Devils would finish the season 2-10, and Coach Franks would be fired the following year after seven games.

The most recent meeting between East Carolina and Duke was the season opener in 2005. What was memorable about this game was that it was the first game under new ECU head coach Skip Holtz. After only three wins in two years, Pirate fans were optimistic that things were going to change. What we saw that day was typical of the Holtz style for the next five years. The Pirates played good offense and very solid defense. The

Skip Holtz era started with a 24-21 win over Duke. Like many other years, the Blue Devils would finish like they started and end the season 1-10.

The University of South Carolina (USC)

The football history between East Carolina and the University of South Carolina could be divided into three parts. Part One would be 1990 and before. Part Two is 1991 through 1999, with Part Three being 2011 through 2021. The games and the results from each part are very different. The one common theme is that most of those games were played in Columbia. In fact, of the twenty games in the series only four were played in Greenville and a neutral site, Bank of America Stadium. Through most of the first 40 years for South Carolina in the Southeastern Conference, winning did not come easy. Since 2000 the Gamecocks have had some genuine success. This success can be linked to big name coaches like Lou Holtz, Steve Spurrier, Will Muschamp and now Shane Beamer.

ECU and South Carolina first met on the football field in 1977, when the Pirates lost a close game 19-16 in Columbia. Beginning in 1984, when the teams met again, South Carolina had their best season in their history up to that point. The Pirates would fall 42-20 and the Gamecocks would finish the regular season 11-1 and lose to Oklahoma State in the Gator Bowl, finishing with a final ranking of No. 11 in the AP poll. Counting that game in 1984, East Carolina and South Carolina would play fourteen times in the next sixteen seasons.

In describing the early history of the series, before 1991, it's safe to say it was all Gamecocks. They won all eight games by an average of 25 points. Those were mostly winning seasons for USC.

Things changed in the Pirates' direction beginning in 1991 and continuing throughout the '90s. The two schools would play seven times from 1991 through 1999 and the Pirates would win five times with four very convincing wins. In the memorable "We Believe" 1991 season, USC made only their second visit to Dowdy-Ficklen Stadium. The game started slowly, with the Gamecocks scoring first. The Pirates took a 10-7 lead into halftime. In the fourth quarter USC scored with just over six minutes remaining to make it 24-20 in favor of ECU. A mistake by the Pirates then backed them up to their own 2-yard line. Jeff Blake threw two passes to get the Pirates to the 29 and then a 71-yard touchdown pass to Hunter Gallimore made the score 31-20 and sealed the win. It would be ECU's first win over South Carolina and the Pirate faithful would tear down the goal posts.

The 1992 ECU/USC game was even closer. The Pirates led 20-18 with 25 seconds remaining in the game. On third down, the Gamecocks attempted a game-winning field goal that was blocked by the Pirates but recovered by the Gamecocks. On fourth down they attempted another field goal that sailed wide, and ECU held on 20-18. Both teams would finish the 1992 season with an identical 5-6 record.

Homecoming in 1994 was not what South Carolina had planned. While neither team would score in the first quarter, ECU would reel off 27 points in six minutes in the second quarter. ECU running back Junior Smith had a great day with 192 yards rushing. The Pirate defense gave up yards and points but ECU spoiled the Gamecocks' homecoming party 52-46.

The teams would meet again in Columbia two years later;

the conditions were different and so was the game. Although it wasn't a tropical storm, rain poured before and during the game. The crowd of 79,000 didn't last, but the Pirate offense did. Scott Harley ran for a then-record 291 yards as the Pirates controlled the game and won easily 23-7. For ECU it would be two wins against the Gamecocks in a row and four wins out of the last five games.

The teams would play again in a much anticipated game in 1997 in Greenville. There was hope that the ECU success since 1991 would continue, but the Pirates never really competed and lost 23-7. Prior to that game, we observed several South Carolina students rummaging through a trash can in the tailgate lot outside the stadium. This went on for a long time. After the game, we concluded they found the ECU playbook in that trash can. This would be the last ECU/USC game played in Greenville until the fall of 2021. This was another much-anticipated game coming after the limited crowds and canceled games of the pandemic. It could not have started better for the Pirates. On the first play of the game an end-around pass by Tyler Snead went for 75 yards and an ECU touchdown. The Pirates scored another touchdown and led 14-7 at the half. The Pirates were up 17-14 with six minutes left in the game when South Carolina kicked a field goal to tie the game at 17. The Pirates quickly went three and out and South Carolina engineered a 4:54 drive, kicking a game-winning field goal as time expired. This was USC's first lead all afternoon and it came on the last play of the game. The 20-17 final score was disappointing considering how well the game started.

The 2016 game in Columbia was another frustrating afternoon. New Pirate coach Scottie Montgomery had won his first two games against Western Carolina and NC State. This game was total domination by the Pirate offense in every statistical category. Quarterback Philip Nelson had 400 yards passing. The Pirates converted 34 first downs compared to only 13 by USC, and ECU dominated the time of possession by 17 minutes with more than 200 yards more total offense. Zay Jones set a school record for catches in a single game. All of this offense only yielded 15 points and one touchdown. Four trips inside the South Carolina 10-yard line did not yield a single point. A fumble, two interceptions, including one from the 1-yard line, and a missed field goal told the story of missed opportunities. ECU simply could not finish a drive. The Pirates would completely outplay the Gamecocks and still lose the game 20-15.

Probably the most interesting game of the series came in 1999. Eastern North Carolina had been devastated by Hurricane Floyd. The Pirate buses were led out of Greenville on back roads to avoid the flooding. More than 82,000 Gamecock fans had gathered to see Lou Holtz' first home game at USC. It was a warm night and the crowd was anticipating a Gamecock win after two losses on the road. The Gamecock fans were disappointed because Steve Logan's Pirates, led by David Garrard and a stout defense, completely controlled the game. The outcome was never in doubt, and the Pirates rolled 21-3. One interesting scene from that game came near the end. One man was sitting there quietly shedding tears of joy. Few people knew that this man, a native of rural South Carolina, was a former ECU player and later coach. Like many of us, he seemed caught up in the emotion of the moment. His name was Ed Emory.

Carl Davis

Florida State University (FSU)

Florida State has a long and varied history. Founded in 1851, it became a college for women in 1905. After World War II, it became coeducational and football was restarted. For almost half of those years, Florida State football was dominated by one man, Coach Bobby Bowden.

ECU and FSU shared the common bond of both schools being independent. The schools played seven times between 1980 and 1990. All but one game was in Tallahassee and Bobby Bowden was the FSU coach for every game. The Seminoles were very good in the '80s, but they were great in the '90s. In that decade they had the best record of any team in college football. It was a true dynasty.

The first seven games with the Seminoles were not even close. Bowden produced a high-octane offense. The Noles outscored the Pirates 348-145. The lowest FSU score in those seven games was 44 points, and that came in 1987 in the only game in Greenville, when the Seminoles won 44-3. That year Florida State would finish 11-1 and win the Fiesta Bowl over Nebraska and finish ranked No. 2 in the polls.

1983 was a little different game for the ECU/FSU series. The game was the season opener for both teams. FSU entered the game and the season ranked No. 7 in the country. As was the norm for FSU, the high-powered offense was in full force, but this time ECU had a high-powered offense of its own. The two teams totaled more than 1,300 yards of offense. For the Pirates, Henry Williams had two returns for a touchdown including a 99-yard kickoff return in the second half. The other return was a 58-yard punt return. It was the only punt by either team all night. Award-winning place kicker Jeff Heath had both a field goal and an extra point blocked. The Seminoles keyed on Heath, who still has the ECU longest field goal record. Two costly fourth quarter turnovers would seal the Pirates' fate. With FSU leading 47-46, the Pirates were driving and just needed a field goal to win. A fumble at the FSU 32-yard line would end the night for ECU.

Coach Emory was not happy with the officiating. There were several very controversial calls that Emory would question. In spite of the loss, a large crowd greeted the team at the Kinston airport. Emory and these Pirates had almost done the impossible.

The Pirates would finish the year 0-3 in the State of Florida. By a total of 13 points, ECU would lose three games to nationally ranked Florida teams, all on the road, including eventual national champion Miami. These would be the only three losses by the Pirates in 1983. Unfortunately, the Pirates would not play in a bowl that year.

The University of Miami (UM)

The University of Miami is one of the elite teams in the history of college football. They have had great coaches, players and teams. They have won a total of five national championships. Only Alabama, Notre Dame and Oklahoma have won more national championships. The coaching legacy at Miami includes Howard Schnellenberger, Jimmy Johnson, Butch Davis, Dennis Erickson, Randy Shannon, Larry Coker, and Mark Richt. Great coaches seem to attract great players. As an example of this, the Miami Hurricanes hold the record for the most players ever drafted in the first round of the NFL draft. For consistency through the years, Miami has had at least one player drafted for forty-eight consecutive years.

East Carolina has generally not fared well against the University of Miami, but there have been some very notable exceptions. Like ECU, Miami was an independent for most of its early years of football prominence. They joined the Big East in 1991 with Virginia Tech, West Virginia, Temple and Rutgers, staying until 2004 when they moved to the ACC. As an independent, besides Florida powerhouse teams like the University of Florida and Florida State, Miami scheduled teams of national note and frequently were in major bowl games.

During the first eight games of this series, ECU was outscored 245 to 68.

The third game of the series in 1983 was an exception to the lopsided scores of the '80s. This was an intense football game. East Carolina held Miami without a score in the first half while getting only a touchdown to lead 7-0 going into the third quarter. This would be the third time in 1983 that the Pirates would lead at the half in Florida. The other two games were at FSU and at Florida. Miami quarterback Bernie Kosar connected for a short pass to put the Hurricanes on the board. ECU blocked the extra point to maintain a 7-6 lead. With under five minutes remaining at the Miami 4-yard line, Jeff Heath attempted a field goal that sailed wide. The Hurricanes moved quickly down the field and Kosar ran it in to make the score 12-7 in favor of Miami. The two-point attempt was unsuccessful, and the Pirates still had a chance. Kevin Ingram drove the Pirates down the field. With four seconds remaining, Ingram attempted a pass to Stephon Adams a few steps from the endzone. The pass appeared to be heading for a wide-open Adams, but just as he was reaching for the ball another ECU receiver hit Adams in his own attempt to get the ball. Time expired and the ball hit the ground. It was a terrible offensive accident by the Pirates. It was called "heartbreaking" by the local paper. Miami would move on and win the National Championship over previously unbeaten Nebraska 31-30 in the Orange Bowl. Twenty years later in a game at the Orange Bowl, I was wearing my ECU shirt when a Miami fan came up and said, "You guys almost cost us the National Championship."

The Pirates would be frustrated by Miami until a Saturday night in 1996 in the Orange Bowl that was broadcast on ESPN. Quarterback Marcus Crandell and running back Scott Harley combined for a smooth performance while the Pirate defense had little trouble with the Butch Davis coached Hurricanes. The Pirates would roll 31-6 in front of a national TV audience.

If you ask most Pirate fans about a game with Miami, the "Hurricane Floyd Game" will be the one they always mention. The storm made landfall in North Carolina on Thursday, September 16, 1999. There was torrential rain and wind accompanied by the usual power outages and flooding common with east coast storms. The East Carolina football team left Greenville the next day for a game in Columbia, South Carolina. Little did they know it would be more than a week before they would return home.

This storm was different from most hurricanes in that it dumped huge amounts of rainfall, especially in the Tar River Basin in and around Greenville and especially further up the river. The storm would do $1.6 billion (1999 USD) of damage in Pitt County alone. Fifty-one people would die in North Carolina, mostly from freshwater flooding. In the days following the storm the rivers rose quickly, and the Tar River would exceed the 500-year flood level. In Greenville, the city was isolated and operating in a state of emergency. With roads impassable, power unreliable, and day-to-day survival often difficult, a football game at Dowdy-Ficklen Stadium was not a priority.

For the football team in Columbia, returning to Greenville was out of the question. USC Coach Lou Holtz loaned the Pirates the use of their facilities for practice. Some local alumni pitched in with food. The coaches bought shorts and underwear at local stores. Miami offered for the game to be played at their home, the Orange Bowl. Not wanting to give up a home-field advantage, the Pirate athletic department arranged for Carter-Finley Stadium to be used since the Wolfpack was on the road that weekend. Seating was first come, first served. The tickets from Dowdy-Ficklen Stadium would admit fans to Carter-Finley. The move worked, and more than 48,000 mostly Pirate fans filed into the stadium. For the players, all week they had seen images of their campus and their city. They had heard stories from friends and family. They knew that after this football game, the hard reality would begin, but first there was a football game to play.

Miami came into the game ranked No. 9 in the country with lots of confidence, highly favored and loaded with stars like Clinton Portis, Kenny Kelly, and Reggie Wayne. From the beginning, it appeared that Miami would roll over the underdog Pirates as expected. The Hurricane offense was dominant in the first half, scoring two touchdowns and two field goals while ECU could only manage a single field goal. The third quarter started poorly for the Pirates as well, as Miami got another field goal to make the score 23-3. ECU running back Jamie Wilson, whose early fumble resulted in a Miami touchdown, ran for 24 yards and scored the first ECU touchdown with less than ten minutes remaining in the third quarter. Wilson would rush for another score with just under twelve minutes remaining in the game to bring the Pirates within six points at 23-17. David Garrard had a good second half, going 20-27 for 222 yards while keeping the ball moving and the Pirates on the field. A Kevin Miller 39-yard field goal brought the Pirates closer, making it 23-20. A bad week for eastern North Carolina ended with a David Garrard-led 79-yard drive and a 27-yard touchdown pass to Keith Stokes. In spite of an impressive 147-yard rushing performance by Clinton Portis, the East Carolina Pirates had scored 24 unanswered points in the second half and beaten the No. 9 Miami Hurricanes. It was as unlikely as ECU playing a home game in Raleigh or beating a team named the Hurricanes after a devastating hurricane. The goalposts came down.

My Miami Travel Log:

Visited South Beach and drove to Key West

Temple University (TU)

Temple is a large public research university located in Philadelphia. Their football history began in 1925, but in athletics Temple is mostly known for men's basketball. In fact, Temple is fifth in the country with wins in basketball. Being part of the Philadelphia "Big Five" makes basketball the most important sport on campus.

Temple's football history, like many other schools, seemed to rise and fall with its coaches. ECU's history with Temple has been up and down, starting with both teams being independent and restarting after almost twenty years with both teams finding their way into the American Athletic Conference. After twenty games, the Pirates hold a slight 11-9 edge in wins.

From 1982 to 1995, ECU dominated Temple by winning eight of eleven games. Most of those games were relatively close with the winning team only having a one- or two-score advantage. The games at Temple in those years were played at Veterans Stadium, the former home of the Philadelphia Eagles and the Philadelphia Phillies. The Owls were a fixture on local television, and this provided more interest in the program while attendance was less-than-stellar.

When ECU landed in the American Athletic Conference, many Pirate fans assumed that most games with Temple would be easy ECU wins. What they failed to realize was that Temple had entered the Matt Rhule era. Coach Rhule put together several of the most successful seasons in Temple's long football history. Matt Rhule's teams played very good defense and were always fundamentally sound. His first season was also Temple's first season in the AAC. While they only won two games, they had the second-best recruiting class in the conference.

The Pirates and Owls met for the first time in almost twenty years in 2014 at Lincoln Financial Field, which had become Temple's new off-campus home that they shared with the Philadelphia Eagles. The Pirates came into the game highly favored with a 6-1 record. Their only loss was by 10 points to South Carolina on the road. It was cold, rainy, and windy on the day after Halloween in Philadelphia, and the game proved to be a horror story for ECU. The Pirates could only score a single field goal until the final three minutes of the fourth quarter. Offensively and defensively, ECU dominated the game, converting 30 first downs to Temple's 10 first downs. The Pirate defense only allowed Temple to gain 135 yards of offense. In spite of playing well on both sides of the ball, ECU had eight fumbles and lost five of them. The Pirates also had twice as many penalty yards. One first quarter fumble was returned for a Temple touchdown. The Owls beat No. 21 ranked East Carolina 20-10. Like so many losses, the Pirates outplayed their opponent everywhere except on the scoreboard.

For me personally, as well, this game was a horror story. My wife and I were in town and I was calling on some customers in downtown Philadelphia while she stayed at the hotel. She fell while getting off a treadmill and could not walk. After a trip to the emergency room with some fine and caring medical professionals, it was determined that her leg was broken and would require surgery to repair it. Happy Halloween! They immobilized the leg and I bought a wheelchair to use on the ride back to North Carolina the next day. We had to pass the stadium on the way heading south on I-95. It was pouring rain. The weather matched our mood. The good news is that she had surgery and made a complete recovery from the broken leg. It did prevent us from traveling to several road games. Thanks to her friends, she was able to make it to all of the remaining home games and to the Birmingham Bowl in a wheelchair. At the bowl game, we sat outside in the rain at Legion Field after I had pushed her up multiple levels of ramps. We both got wet and later the wheelchair started to rust. What a trooper! Less than two weeks later I had the opportunity to attend the very first College Football Playoff game between Oregon and Ohio State at AT&T Stadium in Dallas. We were able to find someone to stay with her for a few days while I went to Dallas. It's incredibly bad form to go to a football game and leave your wife home alone in a wheelchair, but it all started trying to follow the Pirates to Temple.

The next five seasons were all Temple. The Owls' 2015 season saw them go 10-2 in the regular season while losing to Houston in the conference championship game. That season they hosted College GameDay and later that day played the Notre Dame Fighting Irish. It was a close game, with the Irish prevailing 24-20. 2016 saw Temple again win 10 games and Matt Rhule move on. The program he built would continue through two seasons with Jeff Collins.

In the Covid year of 2020, the Pirates went to Philadelphia and brought home a 28-3 victory. The following season in Greenville, the Pirates played against Temple the way Pirate fans were expecting when they joined the AAC. It was a dominant 45-3 win for ECU. In 2022 the Pirates and Owls would play the most exciting game in the series. Temple freshman quarterback E.J. Warner would throw five touchdown passes for 527 yards. ECU's Keaton Mitchell would have his best day as a Pirate rushing for 222 yards and three touchdowns. A late touchdown and a strong defensive stand would seal the win for ECU 49-46. It would be East Carolina's second consecutive winning season.

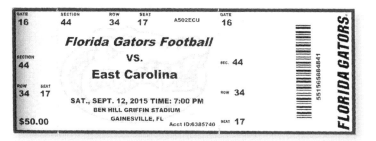

The University of Florida

The Florida Gators are a football institution. They were a founding member of the Southeastern Conference ninety years ago. In its football history, Florida has won eight conference championships and three national championships. The Pirates and Gators have played three times, with the first and second meetings coming 32 years apart.

For ECU, the 1983 Ed Emory-coached team was a special one. They traveled to play all three of the powers in the state of Florida: Miami, Florida State and the Florida Gators. When the Pirates landed in Gainesville for homecoming, the Charlie Pell-coached Gators were ranked No. 5 in the nation. Surprisingly, the Pirates took a 10-7 lead into halftime. In the third quarter, the Gators only scored a field goal to tie the game. In the fourth quarter, Florida scored twice and the Pirates only once to make the score 24-17 in favor of the Gators with less than seven minutes remaining. Four interceptions and two lost fumbles by the Gators really gave the Pirates some golden opportunities during the game. The Pirates drove to the 34-yard line but turned it over on downs. Again, with less than a minute to go, the Pirates could not find a way to score. Florida would win 24-17 and go on to play in and win the Gator Bowl to finish the year 9-2-1 and ranked 6th. The Pirates would end the season ranked No. 20.

Fast forward more than thirty years and the Pirates and Gators would tee it up again, but this time the site was Birmingham. The location was the Birmingham Bowl at the ancient Legion Field. The facility, built in 1926, was showing its age. The 2014 season was the first one for the College Football Playoff, so this bowl was played on January 3, 2015 between the New Year's Day bowls and the CFP Championship. It was a rainy and cool day, but more than 30,000 fans made the trip. The game started well for ECU with a Carden-to-Hardy touchdown pass. It would be the final game for both quarterback Shane Carden and receiver Justin Hardy. Florida would answer with an interception return for a touchdown and two more scores before the half, making the score 21-7 at halftime. The story of the Birmingham Bowl was an ECU team that could move the ball but had trouble scoring. A fumble at the 1-yard line on a quarterback sneak and a missed field goal, both late in the second quarter, set the tone for the rest of the game. For the game, the Pirates had 200 yards more offense than the Gators. It ended 28-20 in favor of Florida and left the Pirates with an 8-5 record.

After not playing each other for more than thirty years, the next time these two teams would meet would be only eight-and-a-half months later in Gainesville. It was pure luck that ECU and Florida had been matched in the Birmingham Bowl with this game scheduled as the second game of the year in 2015. After coming so close in the bowl game, the Pirates had a lot of confidence coming into Gainesville. Shane Carden and Justin Hardy were gone, and a rebuilt team took the field. The Pirates scored first, but the Gators got a touchdown and a field goal to take a 10-7 lead into halftime. The Pirates were able to execute the passing game mostly with Blake Kemp and his three touchdown passes. He pulled ECU to within a touchdown with three minutes remaining and got the ball back with a minute to go for one last drive. Kemp fumbled at the 12-yard line as the clock moved under 20 seconds remaining to end the game. The Pirates moved the ball consistently through the air, but the anemic running game was the difference. ECU totaled -13 yards on the ground. This was just -3 yards from being the all-time worst rushing performance in ECU history. The Gators would go on to win 10 of their first 11 games and finish the season 10-4 and ranked No. 25. The Pirates would finish 5-7 in Ruffin McNeil's final season at ECU.

The summary of the three ECU-versus-Florida games is clear. Each game was decided by only one score. In each game, the Pirates had the ball near the end of the game with an opportunity to score. These are probably not the outcomes that most casual football fans would expect, but the Pirate fans expected more. ECU was always the underdog in every game, but played up the competition with the Gators.

Carl Davis

The University of Pittsburgh (Pitt)

The Pitt Panthers are a legacy football program with a history going back more than 130 years. The Panthers have a long list of famous coaches and players extending back to the early 1900s. Pitt also claims nine national championships, but eight of these are before 1938. They were able to achieve this, including being the consensus national champion in 1976, without conference affiliation. The University of Pittsburgh football program was an independent for 100 years, from1890 to 1990. They became a member of the Big East in 1991 and later moved to the ACC. Being an independent made them a good fit to play ECU in the '80s.

The series started with the Pirates traveling to Pitt in 1984. The game was mostly defense. Pitt was able to get two touchdowns in the first half while the Pirates missed a field goal and let the clock expire at the Pitt 16-yard line to end the half. Ed Emory's team could only get a touchdown and a field goal and fell to the Pitt Panthers 17-10.

Five years later ECU would be back in Pittsburgh, and this time it was all offense by both teams. The Panthers would run the ball effectively with Curvin Richards getting 264 yards on the ground. The Pirates did it through the air with receiver

99

Walter Wilson scoring four touchdowns. ECU would come up short and the game would end with the Pirates at the Pittsburgh 22-yard line. The 15-point underdog Pirates would come close but lose for the second time at Pitt 47-42.

The Panthers made their first trip to Greenville in 1991. This was the most important game in the series. Pitt came to Dowdy-Ficklen Stadium ranked No. 23 while the Pirates were No. 20. With the clock running down with less than four minutes to play and the PIrates trailing 23-16, Jeff Blake engineered a drive to the Pitt 1-yard line. On the next play he would take it to the endzone himself, running to the left and reaching the ball across the goal line with just 46 seconds remaining in the game. East Carolina would go for two points and the win. Again it was Jeff Blake, this time running to the right and diving into the endzone. The Panthers didn't quit and drove the ball to the ECU 11-yard line as time expired. The No. 20-ranked Pirates won 24-23 in what many Pirate fans described as the most exciting game ever played in Dowdy-Ficklen Stadium. It was a high-stakes win after a high-stakes gamble.

The final game in the series would be in 1992 as the Pirates traveled back up to Pittsburgh. It was a very different year, as neither team was ranked or playing particularly well. First-year head coach Steve Logan was trying different approaches. On special teams the week before, the Pirates tried four onsides kicks and a fake punt to beat Cincinnati. Special teams would again determine the outcome of the game against Pitt, who fumbled the opening kickoff and saw the Pirates recover the ball at the 12-yard line to set up the first score of the game. More Pitt miscues led to more Pirate points. A fake punt by ECU kept a drive alive and resulted in another score. When the mistakes ended it was the Pirates winning the game 37-31.

The Pitt series was a good one for ECU. The last two games were against a Panther team that had just joined the Big East. Pittsburgh had a long tradition, and the Pirates always showed up to play them.

ECU VS Tulsa

TULSA

SATURDAY
October 17, 2015
DOWDY-FICKLEN STADIUM
No Readmittance   Date Subject to Change   No Refunds

Account	Price
12580	**$54.00**
Location	Gate
South	**2-3**
Section	Row	Seat
6	**R**	**6**

9142908901163 2

GAME
6

PIRATES
VS.
TULSA

SATURDAY
NOV. 30, 2019

SENIOR DAY
DOWDY-FICKLEN STADIUM

No Readmittance
No Refunds
Date Subject to Change

Account	Price
12580	**$55.00**
Location	Gate
South	**2-3**
Section	Row	Seat
6	**S**	**7**

9143345548099 0

SECTION
102
ROW
9
SEAT
16

7

Conference USA Football
2008 Championship Game
Tulsa vs. East Carolina
H.A. Chapman Stadium

PRICE
$30.00

12/06/2008   11:00am

102

The University of Tulsa (TU)

The University of Tulsa is a very small private university in the football-passionate state of Oklahoma. Tulsa has one of the smallest enrollments of D-1 football schools along with Rice and Wake Forest. The team is the Golden Hurricane. Since they are nowhere near a coastline, the mascot name is not obvious. The name dates back to 1922 when the coach talked about "roaring through opponents." They were planning on using Golden Tornadoes, but learned another school had that name, so the team voted on Golden Hurricane because of the gold jerseys. So, 100 years later the Golden Hurricane is in the middle of the plains.

Tulsa's football tradition is strong. For fifty years they were a mainstay in the Missouri Valley Conference and had regular games with rival Oklahoma State and, to a lesser extent, Oklahoma. Prior to joining Conference USA, like ECU, Tulsa was an independent. They joined CUSA in 2005, eight years after ECU. Prior to CUSA the two teams had met five times starting in the '80s. ECU and Tulsa moved to the American Athletic Conference in the same year. The two schools have met a total of sixteen times, with each team winning eight games. The Pirates won six in a row starting in 2008.

The Golden Hurricane has had some notable coaches. Coaches like Todd Graham, John Cooper and Steve Kragthorpe have walked the sidelines. Former ECU head coach Steve Logan, a native of nearby Broken Arrow, Oklahoma, was an assistant at Tulsa under John Cooper. Current UNC athletic director Bubba Cunningham was the AD at Tulsa prior to coming to Chapel Hill.

Tulsa plays on campus at H.A. Chapman Stadium, formerly Skelly Stadium. It sits adjacent to historic U.S. Route 66. The facility was originally constructed in 1930 and enlarged to seat 40,000 in 1964. It was regularly filled when rivals like Oklahoma State came to play. In 2005 and later 2007, the press box was replaced, club seats were added and seating was reduced to 30,000.

One game with Tulsa that Pirate fans will long remember came on opening day in 2010. It was a Sunday in front of 50,000-plus in Dowdy-Ficklen Stadium in front of a national TV audience. It was also the first game for Coach Ruffin McNeill, who had just replaced Skip Holtz. The game was made for TV and a huge crowd. The teams scored 100 points and generated more than 1,100 yards of offense with almost 800 yards passing. The teams traded touchdowns and field goals, and the Pirates led 17-16 at halftime. The second half can only be described as totally wild. This game had thirteen lead changes! With just 1:22 remaining in the game, Tulsa took the lead once again 49-45. The final drive began on the ECU 34-yard line as quarterback Dominique Davis moved the Pirates down the field. With five seconds remaining and Tulsa in a prevent defense, Davis threw a high strike to 6-foot-8 receiver Justin Jones, jumping among the defenders in the endzone. It was a jump-ball touchdown and game over, with the Pirates winning Ruffin McNeill's first game 51-49.

After the Pirates left the Southern Conference at the end of the 1976 season, they remained as an independent until joining Conference USA in 1997. Lots of Pirate fans thought that ECU would dominate this new conference. That proved not to be the case. In fact, the Pirates never made it to the conference championship game until 2008, twelve years after joining. That game was played on a clear cold Saturday morning in Tulsa. Tulsa quarterback David Johnson came into the game leading the nation in passer rating and the Tulsa team led the nation in yards per game. Johnson threw an interception on the first play of the game, which set the tone for the next sixty minutes. He would throw a total of five interceptions and fumble once. The Pirates were slow and steady without an interception and only one fumble for the entire game. With the score tied at 24 and less than nine minutes remaining in the game, quarterback Patrick Pinkney engineered a seven-minute 53-yard drive that ended with a Ben Hartman field goal. Another ECU interception would end the game and the Pirates won 27-24 and headed for the Liberty Bowl. The Pirates' conference championship was celebrated that day by quarterback Patrick Pinkney and his father Reggie Pinkney, who had celebrated the last ECU conference championship as a member of the Southern Conference team thirty-two years earlier.

University of Cincinnati (UC)

East Carolina has an extensive history with the University of Cincinnati, but that history has been under the radar because of the distance and the fact that the two schools don't share much in common other than being large public institutions. In fact, ECU has played UC twenty-six times since 1986, more than the Pirates have played against any team in that period. In all of East Carolina football history, only three other schools—App State, Southern Miss and NC State—have played more games against the Pirates.

The most unusual stat may be that as of 2022, the Pirates and the Bearcats have played twenty-six times and the Pirates and the Bearcats are all even at thirteen games each. That number is deceiving because ECU won twelve of the first fourteen games and has only won a single game (2017) since 2001. The relative strength of the two programs seems to have flipped. Certainly, with Cincinnati being the first "Group of Five" school to ever make the college football playoff in January, 2022, that separation looks even wider.

The first seven games were all easy ECU wins. The Pirates averaged scoring almost 20 points more than the Bearcats in those early games. The next seven games were much more competitive with Cincinnati winning five out of seven and the scores being much closer.

The Bearcats play in Nippert Stadium on campus. The stadium was built in 1910 with wooden bleachers, but it has been rebuilt and expanded many times now with a club level and luxury suites. It's the fifth oldest college stadium in the country. Cincinnati really hasn't needed a large stadium until the last few years. When the Pirates played there in 1998, the announced attendance was just over 19,000, and that was probably generous. Two days later, a high school football game in Paul Brown Stadium less than three miles away attracted almost 20,000 fans. Although Cincinnati is a medium-size city, the University of Cincinnati has a lot of sports competition from the Cincinnati Reds and the Cincinnati Bengals. Also on the college landscape is Ohio State, just 100 miles away. The image until the last few years as a commuter school has hindered the Cincinnati football image. The only advantage for the Bearcats is recruiting. Ohio is a high school football hotbed, and in recent years Cincinnati has taken full advantage of it.

An example of how the University of Cincinnati football program has changed in the last two decades is from 1998. The Pirates and Bearcats played a November game on a Thursday night on ESPN. Cincinnati came into the game with an 0-8 record, having lost badly all eight times. In fact, the closest loss was by 16 points. The Pirates were lucky to escape with a 24-21 victory. The Bearcats would win their next two games and finish 2-9.

The following year Cincinnati would travel to Greenville and the Pirates would win easily, 48-34. The next game would be in Cincinnati in 2001 and would prove to be a real test for ECU. The Pirates scored first and played an outstanding first half on both offense and defense. For the game, ECU would get more than 300 yards rushing with Leonard Henry rushing for 234 yards. At the half, it was 28-6 with only two field goals by the Bearcats. The second half was very different. Cincinnati seized the momentum and held the Pirates scoreless in the second half while they scored three touchdowns of their own. The final touchdown came with less than five minutes to play. The Bearcats went for two, but were unsuccessful. The Pirates left Nippert Stadium with a close 28-26 win.

The final game between the two schools in Conference USA came in 2004 at Dowdy Ficklen Stadium. The Pirates could only manage 203 yards of offense, but played good defense to keep it close. The Bearcats prevailed 24-19 in John Thompson's second and final season.

The next twenty years would include a decade in which the Pirates and Bearcats would not play. Cincinnati left Conference USA and joined the Big East in 2005, and ECU and UC didn't play again until the Pirates joined the American Athletic Conference in 2014. Those years saw coaches Brian Kelly, Butch Jones and Tommy Tuberville lead the Bearcats with several very good years against improving competition. The Cincinnati program saw plenty of growth under these coaches and in the Big East.

When the two schools finally reconnected it would be in Cincinnati in 2014, the first year for ECU in the American Athletic Conference. It was a wild game and a shootout between two hot offenses. The teams piled up almost 600 yards each. The Bearcats were led by Notre Dame transfer quarterback Gunner Kiel, while the Pirates had senior Shane Carden under center. The game started slowly for the Pirates with two field goals in the first quarter and two touchdowns in the second quarter. This came while Cincinnati piled up 31 points in the first half. The third quarter was even, but the fourth quarter saw an ECU rally. Down 45-34 with less than five minutes left in the game, Shane Carden engineered two touchdown drives and scored to take the lead 46-45 with 1:02 remaining. The Pirate defense couldn't hold Cincinnati and the Bearcats got a field goal and returned an ECU fumble to win the game 54-46. It was a disappointing loss after a great come-from-behind rally. The Pirates would finish the season 8-5 and the Bearcats under Tommy Tuberville would finish 9-4.

The following year was anything but a shootout. In Greenville in 2015, the Pirates were without Shane Carden and the offense struggled to score. The Pirates led 10-0 early in the game and 10-6 at halftime. Cincinnati scored 10 unanswered points and the Pirates tied the game at 16 with more than ten minutes to play. No one could put together a scoring drive until Cincinnati moved the ball in the final minutes and kicked a game-winning 42-yard field goal as time expired. It was a deflating loss for a Pirate team that would finish 5-7 in Ruffin McNeill's final season. The Bearcats would end the season with a bowl loss and a 7-6 record. The first two years in the AAC were two close losses to the Bearcats, but they proved the teams were evenly matched.

There was only one bright spot in the last games with Cincinnati, which came in 2017 in Greenville. Luke Fickell had come to Cincinnati in 2017 to replace Tommy Tuberville. When the Bearcats came to Greenville, they had a 3-7 record while the Pirates under Scottie Montgomery were 2-8. It was an offensive show by quarterback Gardner Minshew and receiver Travon Brown. Brown set both ECU and AAC single-game receiving records with 270 yards. The Pirates started quickly and scored the first three touchdowns. The Pirates would rack up more yards and more points and win easily 48-20. It was the best win of the year for ECU and the only losing season for Luke Fickell.

When the Bearcats came to Greenville in 2021, they were ranked No. 4 in the nation. It was the last regular-season game for both teams. The Pirates were already bowl eligible with a

7-4 record. Surprisingly the Pirates would lead 3-0 at the end of the first quarter, but the talented Bearcats would take control early in the second quarter and coast to a win, 35-13. The 13-0 Bearcats would go on to win the AAC championship and play Alabama in the College Football Playoff. In 2022, although the margin was different Cincinnati would win a close game at home 27-25. It would be the Bearcats thirty second straight home win.

It appears that the football dynamic between UC and ECU has flipped. In the first two decades, the Pirates dominated the Bearcats. That all changed when Cincinnati joined the Big East. The added money from the BCS and the improved competition made a difference. When the two teams got back together as a result of ECU joining the American Athletic Conference, the Pirates were status quo, but the Bearcats were somewhat improved. With more resources, better coaching and better talent, Cincinnati is on its way to becoming an elite team now headed for the Big 12.

Carl Davis

The University of Illinois

Although the University of Illinois is a large public university with more than 50,000 students, the football program has very
little in common with the football program at East Carolina. Illinois has been a member of the Big Ten Conference or its predecessor since 1896. It was one of the founding members of the
Big Ten, the oldest college football conference, but their legacy in
football is not very noteworthy. They have only won four conference championships in more than sixty years. Since ECU was an
independent they were able to pick up some games with Illinois
to fill out the schedule. These were all on the road in Champaign.

The first game in Champaign was in the 1987 season in
front of 62,000 fans. This was definitely a game the Pirates could
have won. Coach Art Baker was frustrated about the loss. The
Fighting Illini were able to capitalize on three ECU turnovers
and turn two of them into scores. A botched field goal by the
Pirates didn't help their cause. The final score was 20-10, and
East Carolina would finish the season a disappointing 5-6.

The next game, again in Champaign, was in the magical
1991 season. We all know that perfect seasons are hard to put
together no matter how good your team is or how lucky you
are. Winning twelve or thirteen games without a loss doesn't

happen often, if at all. This game on August 31, 1991 was as close as East Carolina has ever come to this type of perfection. The Pirates would take an early lead 7-0 on an 88-yard drive that ended when Jeff Blake ran untouched into the endzone. The Illini would answer in a big way. The Pirates could only manage a field goal while Illinois would score 38 points to take a 38-10 lead. This "We Believe" team would answer with three touchdowns of their own. With the score 38-31 and less than two minutes remaining in the game, East Carolina would recover an onside kick at midfield, but be penalized for unsportsmanlike conduct. They could not overcome the first and twenty five in their own territory, and the road trip to start the season ended 38-31. It was a bad start to what would be a great season.

The revenge factor was in play when the Pirates were invited to the Liberty Bowl in 1994 with Illinois as their opponent. This would be the only time the teams would not meet in Champaign. The 7-4 Pirates had a terrible day. Most of the damage was self-inflicted, as ECU would throw four interceptions and lose one fumble. They would be completely shut out on offense while the Fighting Illini would score 30 points. It was a painful end to the 1994 season in Memphis.

The final meeting between East Carolina and Illinois would occur the next season once again in Champlain. Like the 1991 Illini victory, this would be a one-score, 7-point win. Unlike the 38-31 high scoring game from 1991, this game would end 7-0 but again with Illinois as the winner. Robert Holcombe would carry the ball for the Illini a school record forty-nine times. One of those carries would be a 1-yard touchdown which was the winning score and the only score.

The four games with Illinois have all resulted in losses and they all occurred over a seven-year period. They are significant because of the damage to the potential perfect season and the first appearance by the Pirates in the Liberty Bowl.

Syracuse University

Although geographically this is not a natural rivalry, Syracuse and ECU had a good football rivalry for fourteen years. It began with each school as an independent and evolved as Syracuse became a member of the Big East. Syracuse won five of the first seven games, but several of the ECU losses were close contests. The Orange had a habit of recruiting well, had a great coach and ended up nationally ranked in many of those years. In fact they ended the year ranked No. 6 in the AP poll in 1992, a year when they came to Greenville during Steve Logan's first year as head coach. The prior year was the magical Peach Bowl season. The Pirates went north to Syracuse and won that game 23-20.

For me, the most memorable games with the Orange were the last two games that we played in 2000 and 2001. They are memorable for very different reasons. The game in 2000 was memorable for the weather, and the 2001 match-up was played in the Carrier Dome and was memorable for everything but the weather.

The 2000 game, played in Greenville, was a total monsoon. Tropical Storm Helene came ashore across the Florida panhandle and moved across the South. The storm entered

North Carolina the morning before the game. Needless to say, the crowd was affected! In fact, only our SUV was in the White Lot on the south side of the stadium an hour before gametime. ESPN wandered through the area looking for video. They came to us and we gave a good "First Down, Pirates" for the camera. When the game came on the air, they started with a solid green shot of the weather radar screen and talked about the awful weather, but said "Pirate fans are a hardy lot," and cut to the video from behind our car.

It was a steady rain, but we stayed for the whole game. The stadium steps looked like rocks in a mountain stream as the water flowed over them. David Garrard only completed 10 passes that day, but two of them were long passes for touchdowns. Special teams blocked a punt, Leonard Henry ran for more than 100 yards and the defense played very well. The Pirates won easily 34-17. It was a total team win. The announced crowd of more than 33,000 was less than 10,000 by the end of the game.

Many times in the last twenty years, people have asked about the best game, best crowd, best player, etc. Our trip to Syracuse in 2001 was the strangest. It had a lot of twists and turns and plenty of unexpected moments.

To begin, the game at Syracuse was originally scheduled to be played on September 15, four days after the terrorist attacks. With flights canceled and with emotions at an all time high, the game was postponed until September 29. We had originally planned to fly to the game, but couldn't rebook our flight so we decided to just drive the more than 600 miles to western New York. Driving was the beginning of the adventure.

We arrived at our hotel in Syracuse on Friday afternoon. The folks at the hotel told us about a wonderful Italian festival going on downtown. We decided to drive downtown and enjoy the festival and have dinner. On the way, there was literally an explosion under the hood of my car. Smoke and water poured out. I learned later that the water pump had seized and the belt that connected everything under the hood came flying apart. It was one big mess. The tow truck driver picked up the car and then took us to the hotel. This was not a good start to the weekend. I'm sure the Italian food was good, but we never found out for ourselves.

The next morning the repair shop said that they had found a water pump and a belt and miraculously we could be on our way in plenty of time for the game. In the pre-Uber days, we took a cab to the car shop. Unfortunately, the car was not ready, but the mechanic said, "Hey, you can take my car," and tossed me the keys. Seeing his car and hearing the sound it made when I started it, I had serious doubts we could make it three miles to the Carrier Dome. My wife called it a piece of junk. I had stronger words. We got there in plenty of time, but our ECU friends told us that our BMW would be long gone by the time the game was over.

There was another problem even before the game began. The Carrier Dome was the largest domed stadium on a college campus, but the rows of seats were not the same length. The sections are pie-shaped and we were seated on a very short row of only six seats. Just before the national anthem, four very large people came into our row. We stood in the aisle to allow them into the row, then we continued to stand there during the playing of the national anthem. When we turned to sit down, the four fans in our row were now occupying all six seats. Fortunately the ECU section was not full; Coach Logan's wife was sitting several rows below us, and we moved down and sat with her.

After the long drive, the car mishap, and losing our seats, the game was even more strange. It wasn't even the football game. It was what happened to Conference USA referee Gerry Bram.

The game was competitive from the very beginning. While Syracuse took a 20-10 lead at halftime, the Pirates scored the next two touchdowns to take a 24-20 lead midway through the third quarter. Syracuse scored again, but the Pirates answered on a 33-yard pass from David Garrard to make the score 30-29. Then the unexpected happened. Back judge Gerry Bram was standing near the ECU sideline and simply fell over. Coach Logan signaled the Syracuse sideline. What happened in the next ten or fifteen minutes seemed like hours. Paramedics rushed onto the field and immediately determined that his heart had stopped and he wasn't breathing. The 36,000 fans in the Carrier Dome were completely quiet. It was so quiet you could hear the medical folks talking on the field. Each time they shocked him, you could clearly see his body jerk and the crowd would quietly groan. After a few minutes, he was put into an ambulance and taken from the field. At that moment no one knew if he survived, but he did! He had a lucky heart attack because help was forty yards away, the Syracuse team physician was a cardiologist, and the medical center was a few blocks from the Carrier Dome. The next season, Gerry Bram was introduced to the Syracuse crowd with a standing ovation at the first home game of the year.

After all of the emotion of that moment, it seemed that the air had been sucked out of the Carrier Dome. Syracuse scored on the next drive and scored once again to win the game. In a lot of ways, the last part of the game didn't seem to matter. It was a long drive home in our repaired car and an end to one of our most memorable football weekends.

The University of Memphis (U of M)

The University of Memphis is a large state-supported university that many folks remember as Memphis State. Like ECU, the University of Memphis began as a teacher training school. Memphis is one of only two schools in America with a live tiger mascot. Most recently Tom IV has been housed at the Memphis Zoo. Like the University of Cincinnati and Louisville, Memphis has a very strong basketball culture. While football is important, basketball is more dominant. With Penny Hardaway as the Tigers coach, basketball has recently become even more important at Memphis.

The Tigers play in the Liberty Bowl in the midtown section of the city. The stadium was built in 1963 in a successful attempt to lure the annual Liberty Bowl game from Philadelphia. It was built on the now-defunct fairgrounds. It has been renovated many times and now seats 58,000 but still looks dated.

The ECU and Memphis series started more than 30 years ago. The Pirates have been mostly dominant, winning more than two-thirds of the twenty-five games. The teams split the first four games in the early '90s. In the early 2000s, Memphis won four out of five games. Other than 2017 and 2018, the Pirates have won every game against the Tigers beginning in

2006. Like the Pirates, the Tigers were mostly independent until joining Conference USA in 1996, where they remained until joining the AAC in 2012. There were not many successful seasons for Memphis through most of their football history. In fact, prior to 2003, the Tigers had only been to one bowl game. That quickly changed with Coach Tommy West and later Justin Fuente and Mike Norvell.

With the jump to the American Athletic Conference two years before the Pirates and the fact that the teams were in different divisions, the Pirates and Tigers have only met four times in the past ten years. 2017 and 2018 were both losses by the Pirates to good Tigers teams under Mike Norvell. In 2021 and 2022, the teams played the most memorable games in the history of the series.

The 2021 Pirates headed to Memphis with bowl eligibility on the line after six long years. The Tigers were also playing their 10th game of the year and also seeking bowl eligibility. ECU dominated this game on offense. They dominated yardage, had twice as many first downs and dominated time of possession 42 to 17 minutes. The only place the Pirates couldn't dominate was on the scoreboard.

The teams traded touchdowns in the first quarter while the second quarter saw the Pirates put together several good drives which ended in three made field goals. One drive was 13 plays and another was 19 plays. Memphis scored a touchdown but the extra point failed. Their kicking would become a theme later in the game. The score was 16-13 Pirates at the half. The third quarter was back and forth with each team turning the ball over until Memphis broke through for a touchdown and the lead. The Pirates had one last drive in the fourth quarter that ended in a Rahjai Harris touchdown with 1:32 left in the game, and with the extra point they led 23-20. Memphis had one last chance and put together a 15-play 75-yard drive that ended as time expired with a field goal to tie the game at 23 and send it into overtime. ECU had the ball first on offense, and on the second play Keaton Mitchell ran for 24 yards and a score. After a successful extra point, it was up to Memphis to answer. And they did. A short pass and a 20-yard run, and the Tigers were within a point at 30-29. Coach Houston called a timeout to not only ice the kicker, but to prepare for a possible two-point conversion. And that's what transpired. Memphis went for the win and the two-point conversion, but the Pirates had the perfect defense with maximum pressure on the quarterback. The pass failed and the Pirates won 30-29 and became bowl-eligible for the first time since 2014.

When I began writing about the ECU-versus-Memphis series, there didn't seem to be many compelling stories. In fact, prior to 2021, the two teams had not played a close game for more than fifteen years. The overtime win by the Pirates in 2021 was just a prelude to the following season. In 2022 the Pirates had stumbled to a surprising 3-3 record. Memphis was 4-2 after blowing a huge lead the previous week. The Tigers took a 10-0 lead early in the second quarter and after a failed fake punt on fourth and 24 by the Pirates, they drove for another touchdown. At that point and down 17-0, ECU seemed to find some life and answered with their first touchdown. After a Malik Fleming interception and short touchdown drive, the Pirates made it 17-13 at the half. The Pirates seized the momentum in the third quarter with a Julius Wood interception and return for a touchdown. The teams would trade field goals in the fourth quarter, and it appeared the Pirates had the game in control with a Keaton Mitchell touchdown with less than two minutes remaining, but Tiger quarterback Seth Henigan led a quick drive for a touchdown and the teams headed to overtime. In the first OT, the teams would trade touchdowns and extra points. In the second overtime, the teams would each score a touchdown and fail on the two-point conversion. Overtime number three would see both teams successfully scoring two-point conversions with ECU's Keaton Mitchell dashing to the endzone after catching a short Holton Ahlers pass. Finally in overtime number four, a blitz by Memphis would allow Holton Ahlers to throw a short fade to CJ Johnson in the endzone, and the answer by the Tigers sailed out of the endzone. Finally after years of less than competitive games, the 2021 game would end in overtime and 2022 would end with four overtimes. The four overtimes made that contest the longest game in ECU history.

My Memphis Travel Log:

Visited Graceland and walked down Beale Street

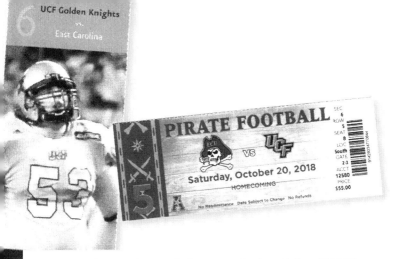

The University of Central Florida (UCF)

The Knights of the University of Central Florida are a unique story. The University of Central Florida is one of the largest universities in the country with more than 70,000 students. It has only been in existence for fifty-eight years, half as long as East Carolina. The campus is simply huge and is located about fifteen miles outside downtown Orlando. Everything looks new and looks like Florida.

No mention of UCF football can be made without a discussion of their stadium. Since the school was relatively new when football began at UCF in 1979, the team played in the Citrus Bowl Stadium in Orlando. This was fifteen miles from campus and created all the same issues that other schools have with off-campus facilities. The current stadium was built on campus and opened in 2007, and the Pirates played there for the first time in 2008. The stadium was originally named Bright House Networks Stadium. The university sold the naming rights to the local cable and internet provider. The stadium is a steel skeleton structure, but everything else is aluminum. The floor, the seats, the aisles, and the stairs all are shiny aluminum. Early in the history of the stadium, there was significant lightning in the area while the Pirates were playing the Knights. No attempt was made to stop the game in the aluminum stadium by either the officials or the coaches. The effect of this construction is that when the crowd is jumping up and down, the entire stadium shakes. It was known as the "Bounce House." TV cameras show a shaky image. An attempt was made to reinforce the stadium to lessen this effect. While there was some improvement, it still shakes. When the naming rights deal expired, the stadium was officially named "Bounce House Stadium."

The football history at UCF is only forty-three years, less than half as long as ECU. The football program began in 1979 in Division III. After only three years in Division III, UCF spent eight years in Division II and then six years in FCS. The Knights were independent in FBS until joining the MAC in 2002 and then moving to Conference USA in 2005. The Pirates had a long headstart in Conference USA, joining in 1999. ECU and UCF played four times in the 1990s prior to joining C-USA, when both schools were independent. The Pirates won all four games, and only one game was decided by one score. ECU outscored UCF 139-69 in those games. ECU had a large head start in football.

It's impossible to really look at UCF football history without a long look at George O'Leary. He had a strong record at Georgia Tech and then there was a scandal about his hiring at Notre Dame. Three years later and a year before joining C-USA, he was announced as the new coach at UCF. O'Leary would go 0-11 in his first year with the Knights. Controversy followed him to UCF when a player collapsed and died during practice. While the school was initially found guilty, upon appeal the athletic department was cleared. His twelve seasons would yield some good teams and four conference championships. He would end his career as UCF's most winning coach, but his record against the Pirates was 4-5.

There were two very dramatic games between the Pirates and the Knights during the George O'Leary era. The first game was in 2008 and it was dominated by the two defenses. The Knights led 10-0 at the half but the Pirates rallied and scored the game-tying touchdown with just under two minutes remaining in the game. The two teams traded a fumble and an interception in the final 33 seconds, and it went to overtime. ECU's Emanuel Davis picked off a pass on the first play of overtime. This allowed Ben Hartman to kick the game-winning field goal, and the Pirates won in Orlando 13-10.

The next year was another Pirate win under Coach Skip Holtz, 19-14, but not as close as the final score would show. The 2014 season under Ruffin McNeill was a year of high expectations after going 10-3 the year before. The Pirates would end 2014 with a highly anticipated game with UCF on the first Thursday night in December. It was a national TV game on ESPN. The Pirates had won eight games coming into December. While the game was tied 6-6 after the first quarter, the Knights poured it on in the second quarter and took a 23-9 lead into the half. They added another field goal and they led 26-9 in the fourth quarter. That's when the Shane Carden comeback began. Three Carden touchdown passes would give the Pirates the lead with just over two minutes remaining in the game. Unfortunately, lots of ECU fans had left at the beginning of the quarter, believing that the game was decided.

After the last Pirate touchdown, UCF used only 30 seconds before turning the ball back over to the Pirates on downs with 1:47 remaining. ECU used 1:37 and gave up 20 yards on four plays. The Knights had 10 seconds to play on their own 35-yard line. A 14-yard sideline pass consumed seven seconds but put UCF in a position for a Hail Mary pass to reach the endzone, and that's what happened. A 51-yard desperation pass sailed over the hands of two ECU defenders and into the hands of UCF's Breshad Perriman, who was standing in front of another ECU defender two yards deep in the endzone. The deafening roar of the crowd immediately turned to silence as the Pirates gave up the game on the last play, 32-30. It was a crushing loss for Shane Carden and the seniors playing their last game at Dowdy-Ficklen Stadium. It was made especially painful after the spectacular three-touchdown comeback in the fourth quarter. To many who watched the inspired comeback, it was the most shocking loss ever at Dowdy-Ficklen Stadium.

For the Knights the 2014 season, although a good 9-4 year, was a significant step back from their 12-1 season in 2013 that included a win over Baylor in the Fiesta Bowl. The 2015 season was very different. By the time the Pirates arrived in Orlando, UCF had lost the first ten games of the year and George O'Leary had resigned two weeks earlier. This was less than two years after their Fiesta Bowl victory. Like the year before, this was another AAC Thursday night game. UCF took the opening kickoff and moved down the field for a touchdown. That would be it for their scoring. The Pirates would simply dominate the game on offense and defense. Quarterback Blake Kemp led the team to five touchdowns and 622 yards of total offense. The defense did their part and only allowed UCF 161 yards after the first drive. It was an easy Pirate win, 44-7 in an otherwise difficult year.

The next five years would be dominated by UCF. The Knights easily won all five games by an average margin of over 24 points. 2018 saw the Knights go 12-1, with the only loss being in the Fiesta Bowl, and finishing No. 11 in the polls. Scott Frost had succeeded George O'Leary and in just his second year, 2017, he led UCF to a perfect 13-0 record and a win in the Peach Bowl. Unfortunately, they would not be included in the college football playoff in spite of their perfect record.

In 2021, ECU traveled to Orlando to face the 2-2 Knights. The Pirates were playing well and sat at 3-2. This would be

Coach Gus Malzhan's first season at UCF. The teams were evenly matched. For the game, ECU had only one more yard of offense than UCF, 360 to 359. The teams were so evenly matched that defense dominated the first half as both teams could only manage a field goal in the second quarter; the score was 3-3 at halftime. The Pirates moved ahead with a touchdown late in the third and added on in the fourth with a field goal. Late in the fourth quarter a UCF field goal cut the margin to three points. The Pirates could not move the ball and went three-and-out. The Knights engineered an agonizing, time-consuming, 11-play, 64-yard drive scoring from one yard out with only 23 seconds left in the game. UCF would win 20-16.

2022 was a much different story. Despite being a five point underdog, the Pirates took a 17-3 lead at the half. While the defense gave up yardage, they did not give up many points. Three interceptions and a forced quarterback fumble were the big difference in the game. The Pirates game plan worked perfectly producing a 34-13 win.

The history between ECU and UCF spans twenty one games, with the Pirates winning eleven of them. The Pirates won eight of the first nine games, while the Knights have won nine of the last twelve. With UCF heading to the Big 12, it's doubtful that there will be much more history written with these two schools. The Pirates did send the Knights off to the Big 12 with a signature win in 2022.

My UCF Travel Log:

Visited various Disney World and Universal Studios parks and experienced lots of other Orlando attractions

Tulane University

The football culture of Tulane University and East Carolina University could not seem more different, but for some unexplained reason the teams seem to mesh. First, Tulane is an old, private university in a medium-size city. Second, they have half as many students as ECU. There is a long football history at Tulane including membership in the Southern Conference, thirty years in the SEC and later thirty years as an independent. The Green Wave landed in Conference USA one year before ECU in 1996 and moved to the American Athletic Conference in 2014 along with ECU. Maybe the two similar conference moves and multiple common opponents have helped form a bond. LSU is their biggest rival with 98 games between the two teams but no games in the last 10-plus years.

Winning seasons are not the norm at Tulane. The exception was in 1998 in their second year in C-USA, when Coach Tommy Bowden led them to a perfect 12-0 season including a win in the Liberty Bowl as the Conference USA champion. They would finish the year ranked No. 7 in the nation, but were locked out of a BCS bowl opportunity. The way scheduling in C-USA was done, ECU and Tulane did not meet in 1998. The Pirates have done well against Tulane in the last three decades and hold a

12-7 victory margin over the Green Wave.

For 48 years Tulane played football at Tulane Stadium on campus, which was also the original home of the New Orleans Saints and the Sugar Bowl. When the stadium was closed in 1974, Tulane moved into the new Louisiana Superdome. While it's an excellent NFL-class facility, the Tulane crowd seemed to be swallowed by the size. While crowds were announced in the 14,000-15,000 range in the last two years in the dome, the real numbers were half of that. Not being on campus really hurt school spirit and student attendance. In the same year that Tulane joined the AAC, they opened a brand-new stadium on campus, Yulman Stadium. While the crowds have improved, they are still small, but the atmosphere is much better. The on-campus location allows for tailgating which seems to help the game-day atmosphere.

In 2008 after big wins over two ranked teams, Virginia Tech and West Virginia, the Pirates traveled to the Superdome to take on Tulane. The Pirates were ranked No. 14 and were heavily favored. It was a surprising game for both teams. The Pirate offense sputtered and Tulane forced four costly turnovers, all inside the ECU 40-yard line. The only ECU score in the first half came from a CJ Wilson blocked field goal attempt that was returned for a touchdown by linebacker Quentin Cotton. The first ECU turnover, inside the ten, was turned into Tulane's first score. A 24-yard touchdown pass from Patrick Pinkney to Jamar Bryant with 1:41 remaining in the game put the Pirates ahead for good. The Pirates would win the game 28-24 and would drop one spot in the AP Poll to No. 15. This would be a case of winning the battle and losing the war. The Pirates lost senior left tackle Stanley Bryant and senior linebacker Quentin Cotton to injuries in this game, and both players were out for the season. It would be a bad turning point in a season that started out so well.

By far the most frustrating game in this series came in 2013. Ruffin McNeill's team was a heavy favorite heading for the Superdome. In the game, six trips by the Pirates into the red zone only yielded four field goals and a touchdown for 19 points. On one of those red zone trips, Shane Carden was intercepted and it was returned for Tulane's only touchdown in regulation. Carden would throw for 480 yards and the Pirates would dominate with 233 yards more offense than Tulane. The Pirates' only touchdown, which tied the game, came with 1:48 remaining in the game. Still the Pirates got the ball back, drove down the field and missed a 42-yard field goal that would have won the game. The teams traded touchdowns in the first two overtimes. In the third overtime, ECU missed a field goal and the game ended with Tulane on top 36-33. It was a game of multiple missed opportunities.

In 2017 in Greenville, the two teams again went to overtime. This was after ECU scored 10 unanswered points in the fourth quarter. The Green Wave scored a touchdown and stopped the Pirates on fourth down to win 31-24. Even with a Pirate win in 2021, Tulane has won four of the last five games. The game in 2022 was typical of the recent games. Over 400 yards in total offense only yielded nine points. Moving the ball is not the problem for ECU when they face Tulane, but scoring is difficult.

It is not surprising that Tulane has historically struggled with the Pirates. They have had numerous losing seasons since the teams first met in 1991, and generally the Pirates have taken advantage until the last few years.

My Tulane travel log:

Visited Bourbon Street, ate at great restaurants and listened to live music throughout the French Quarter

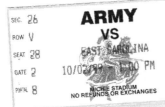

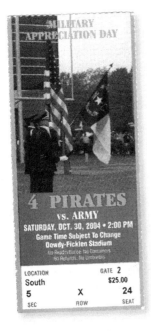

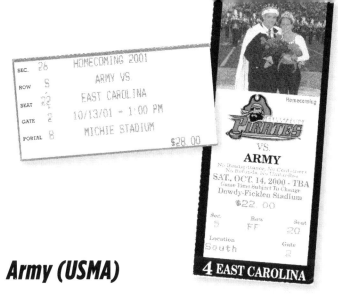

Army (USMA)

When you talk about special football places, the U.S. Military Academy at West Point has to be near the top of the list. It's special there, not for the quality of the game on the field, but for just about everything else. It is a different football game in a very different place.

Over the course of many years when I talk about our football trips, people often ask the question about our favorite place to travel for games. My response is that from a total experience, a trip to the U.S. Military Academy is the best. We always flew to New York and made a four-day weekend out of our trips. It started with shopping in the city and dinner and maybe a show. If you like New York, the fall is a great time to visit. Our trip continued on Saturday morning, when early on game day a bus would pick us up at the hotel and take us to a pier on the Hudson River. We would board a 150-foot yacht with a hundred other Pirate fans, have breakfast and plenty of adult Pirate beverages and sail up the river. I supplied the Pirate flag. It takes several hours to make the 35-mile trip, but the scenery is outstanding, especially when the fall colors are at their best.

Michie Stadium is old, but that doesn't tell the story. It was built almost a hundred years ago in one of the most scenic spots on any college campus. The stadium sits next to a reservoir on a bluff high above the Hudson River. They use school buses to transport fans who arrive by boat up the steep winding road to the stadium. It was named for a cadet who helped start football at West Point and was killed in 1898 in the Spanish-American War.

Most modern fans don't seem to appreciate the history of Army football. They have three consecutive national championships and a number of All-Americans from their heyday era of the 1940s. This is by far one of the most tradition-rich venues for college football. The Naval Academy is similar, but the Army experience is enhanced by the beautiful setting.

The day at Army begins with a parade on campus. The game itself starts with the entire Corps of Cadets marching into Michie Stadium. Of course, the game ball and the flags are brought in by cadets parachuting to the 50-yard line. They, of course, land where they are supposed to land. After the pregame ceremonies, the cadets take their place in the stadium. As you may have seen at the Army-Navy game, the entire Corps of Cadets stands throughout the entire game. They have synchronized cheers and sing together at certain moments. They have a great time. Usually the outcome of the game determines whether they get leave that weekend.

While a lot of schools, including ECU, have a cannon to fire when their team scores and at other important moments. Army has a CANNON! On the field, they have a small old field-artillery-type cannon, but it just fires to signal the real cannons. On a bluff across the river and across the valley, they have several howitzers ready to fire. They fire six rounds for a touchdown. In the stadium, several miles away, across the river the earth shakes! It is a very impressive salute. When ECU had a big lead, our fans were hoping Army would score just to hear those cannons!

East Carolina and Army have played eight times, four at home and four in West Point, with ECU winning all eight. A few of those games were decided by less than a touchdown, but in reality those were mostly not competitive games. Army was overmatched. This was all within a ten-year period. As most people understand, recruiting football players to the U.S. Military Academy is not easy.

A lot of fans have wondered and commented about Army using timeouts near the end of the game when they are down by many touchdowns and the outcome has long been decided. There is sometimes booing and worse from the opposing fans. There is an important lesson here. Army doesn't quit, no matter what. Even if it's hopeless, Army will fight until the clock shows nothing but zeros. That's what they teach at the U.S. Military Academy. That's what we, as Americans, expect of our cadets and our Army.

While football is important but different at West Point than at other schools, when it comes to the Army-Navy rivalry, it goes to a different level. This is one of the biggest rivalries in sports, but what makes it different is that the outcome of the game usually has no significance in the rankings or postseason play.

After every game, the Army players all quietly and reverently stand in front of the Corps of Cadets with helmets in their hands, and together they sing the Army alma mater. On our last trip, a number of Army fans were very complimentary of the fact that our ECU players stood with the Army team with helmets in hand for this moment. It was a classy show of respect by East Carolina that was appreciated by Army. Sportsmanship was on display that day, as it is most days in West Point.

Our trips to West Point have ended like they started, on a yacht sailing down the Hudson back toward New York. As the sun sets, we have a great dinner, lots of Pirate beverages and finally sail into New York Harbor. The yacht turns toward the Statue of Liberty and everyone gets a great view. It's a fitting end to a trip to Army and West Point.

The Army experience in West Point doesn't end when you get back to New York City or even when you return home. For many days after the game, the fight song, "On, Brave Old Army Team", keeps playing in your head. They use it for every score, every defensive stop, every first down, probably thirty times a game. Although you can't get it out of your head, you really don't try because like the entire Army experience, it's a good one.

My Army Travel Log:

Saw the sights in New York City
Toured the campus at West Point

University of Houston

The Houston Cougars are a great study of college football in a major city. In spite of the disadvantages of a dilution of sports fans in a major metro area of seven million people, they have flourished. They have used their large alumni base and have leveraged that base in the football-crazy state of Texas. While there are still plenty of Longhorn and Aggie fans in southeastern Texas, the Cougars have become the local college team for basketball and more recently football. They have done what Temple, the University of South Florida, Tulane, and others have so far failed to do.

The Cougars were in the Southwestern Conference and had a legendary coach, Bill Yeoman. He was innovative and got the team into the top ten four times and the top five twice. Like many schools in the conference in that period, there was controversy about recruiting, paid players and similar issues. While they had success after Coach Yeoman, the NCAA stepped in with sanctions in 1991. Only three winning seasons followed until 2006. The last decade has seen a resurgence in the program, and the fans have returned in force.

After the success of Coach Guy Lewis in the early 1980s with Phi Slama Jama, the Cougar basketball program fell on hard times. Like the football program competing with professional football in the same city, Houston basketball was competing with the Houston Rockets of the NBA. It seems that football and basketball success at the University of Houston has been in parallel. In basketball, Houston has done what many schools have done in football; they made their basketball arena smaller. They have gone from over 10,000 seats, to 8,500, to now just 7,100. Those 7,100 fans are treated to an exceptional experience. The entire interior of the arena has been demolished and renovated at a cost of more than $60 million.

In 2013, the University of Houston began construction of a new $120 million football stadium with a capacity of 40,000 fans. It was constructed on the site of the original Robertson stadium that was built during World War II. In the '90s and early 2000s, the lack of success showed in the old Robertson Stadium.

My first football trip to Houston was in October 1999. The most notable thing on that first trip was the students, or rather the lack of them. Since we had never been there, we were a little lost. I knew that Robertson Stadium was on the campus, but I didn't see any signs. There was no traffic to follow! I didn't see any tailgating either. I pulled up in front of the student union building and saw two coeds walking down the sidewalk. I rolled down the window and asked, "Excuse me ladies, but do you know where the football stadium is?" They slowly looked at each other and back toward our car and said, "Sir, we are sorry but we don't." If our rental car had a sunroof, we could have seen the stadium lights from the student union. We were just two blocks east of the stadium. That lack of student support showed at the game as well. There was an announced crowd of 14,000 but that was more than double the number of fans actually in the seats. The student section had about 300 students when the game started and fewer in the second half.

It was a defensive game. Houston had beaten UNC-CH in Chapel Hill and had a 4-3 record with a loss to Alabama. David Garrard threw for one touchdown and ran for another. The Pirate defense was terrific. Kevin Monroe had two interceptions and Anthony Adams had an interception and a return for a touchdown. The final score was 19-3 Pirates. Who said Steve Logan was just an offensive coach? The next season in November 2000, the game ended when ECU safety John Williamson intercepted a pass. Williamson ran six yards and took a knee without scoring. ECU was up 62-20, and the Logan offense and quarterback David Garrard had their highest offensive output of the season.

East Carolina's history with Houston is almost evenly divided, with the Cougars winning nine and the Pirates winning seven games. ECU was more dominant in the beginning of the series winning four of the first five games. Houston has won four of the last five. There have been several games that were very memorable for Pirate fans.

After the 62-20 rout in Greenville in 2000, the Pirates and Cougars didn't play again until two years later in Houston in November 2002. For those few ECU fans in the stands that day, this was one game that is hard to forget. Despite giving up 300 yards rushing to the Cougars' running back, the Pirates—with Paul Troth at quarterback and Art Brown carrying the ball—rallied in the fourth quarter from a 17-point deficit to tie the game with less than three minutes to play. The defense held, and the game went into the first overtime. Troth threw a 4-yard pass to tie the first overtime and a 20-yard pass to Richard Alston to put the Pirates ahead in the second overtime period. In overtime number three, Travis Heath forced a Houston fumble and on the first play of ECU's possession, Art Brown took it 25 yards for the Pirate win, 54-48.

The game in Houston in 2011 was beyond disappointing.

The Pirates started slowly and could only manage a field goal for the entire game. We happened to be sitting near the coaches' wives. At halftime, an ECU assistant coach's wife leaned over the wall behind the Pirate bench and yelled, "Get your shit together. This is embarrassing. We have family here!" It was embarrassing as the Pirates lost 56-3.

In 2022, the Pirates were favored in Greenville. After a disappointing loss in Cincinnati, the ECU offense could not score and the defense gave up yards and points. In Coach Mike Houston's worse loss the Cougars would win easily 42-3.

The 2017 ECU-Houston game, played in Houston, was an example of much of that season and the previous two years. The Pirate offense really played well, but the defense was simply overmatched. The statistics are very, very telling. In time of possession, the Pirates dominated and held the ball for more than 40 minutes, a two-to-one ratio. Gardner Minshew set the ECU single-game record for completions with 54. Where it mattered, on the scoreboard, Houston won 52-27. In spite of losing by four scores, total yardage was in the Pirates' favor! ECU's drives were long and methodical with three turnovers mixed in, while Houston's drives were quick. Sitting next to Gardner Minshew's father, I could sense the frustration as his son did a great job leading the offense. The ECU offense knew they had to score on every possession, because the defense could not stop Houston. They knew they were fighting a losing battle.

Then there was the Case Keenum era at Houston. The Pirates were 2-2 against Keenum, but won the game that mattered the most. Coach Kevin Sumlin arrived at Houston just before Keenum's sophomore year. His timing was good, just like his move immediately after Keenum's graduation to Texas A&M, where Johnny Manziel was starting his redshirt season. As a friend said about Case Keenum, "How much eligibility does he have? Seems like he's been there for eight years."

Houston's first game with Case Keenum at quarterback against ECU was a nail-biter. Keenum threw two interceptions that set up touchdowns, and then was replaced by quarterback Blake Joseph. A blocked field goal by C.J. Wilson and return by Zack Slate set up another score. Chris Johnson had a good game with two touchdowns, but the end was lucky for East Carolina. Down 37-35, the Cougars missed two field goals in the final two minutes, either of which could have won the game. Keenum had two good games against the Pirates, winning 41-28 in 2008 and that blowout 56-3 in 2011.

When it counted most, in the Conference USA championship game in Greenville in 2009, Case Keenum just couldn't quite pull off the win. In the only conference championship game played in Dowdy-Ficklen Stadium, Keenum was good, almost great. The Cougars were ranked No. 18 coming to Greenville. They cut the lead to 38-32 with less than four minutes to play. Keenum ended with 56 completions, two shy of the all-time NCAA record. With 42 seconds remaining, Keenum threw into the west endzone and the ball bounced off the shoulder pad of ECU defender Travis Simmons and into the arms of Pirate Van Eskridge. The Pirates were conference champs for the second straight year.

My UH Travel Log:

Toured NASA Headquarters in nearby Kemah, Texas

UAB VS

Coach McNeill
2010-current

$45

Record: 19-19
DFS Record: 12-6

SATURDAY
November 16, 2013
DOWDY-FICKLEN STADIUM
No Readmittance   Date Subject to Change   No Refunds

Location		Gate
South		**2-3**
6	**V**	***1**
Section	Row	Seat

91432078287857

EAST CAROLINA

SEC	ROW	SEAT

Suite 12

94 BRYANT TURNER

UAB FOOTBALL 20 10

GAME 5
vs. EAST CAROLINA
NOVEMBER 11 at LEGION FIELD

SEC	ROW	SEAT

Suite

SECTION		
37		
ROW		
18		
SEAT		
1		
PRICE		
$0.		

UAB Blazers
vs
East Carolina
Saturday Sept. 9th 2006 6PM
Legion Field

The University of Alabama at Birmingham (UAB)

The University of Alabama at Birmingham would be described by many in the sports world as the Rodney Dangerfield of college football. As an educational institution, UAB is a proven leader, with five health sciences including medicine and dentistry. The University of Alabama at Birmingham is affiliated with one of the largest hospital systems in the country and is the largest employer in the state of Alabama. Academic success, however, has not translated to success in football.

Football didn't begin at UAB until 1991. It was a struggle in many ways, especially in the large shadows created by Alabama and Auburn. Without their own stadium, UAB has been forced to play in the old Legion Field. Attendance has been poor and the shabby conditions at Legion Field seem to make it worse. Announced attendance in the '90s and 2000s was always between 10,000 and 20,000, but the real numbers were much lower. In fact, on one of the last trips by ECU to play at UAB, three of us got together to actually count the number of people in the stadium. We divided the stadium into thirds, counted the people, and added the numbers. It was less than 800. Needless to say, it was the worst attended college football game I have ever seen.

The game against the UAB Blazers in 1999 was very memorable for a number of reasons, most of them bad. First of all, this was the second year in a row we had played at Legion Field, because we had faced the University of Alabama there in 1998. This time it was in front of 70,000 empty seats while the year before against Alabama there were very few empty seats. The announced crowd was 18,000 against UAB, but that was more than double the number of folks in the stands that afternoon. Secondly, the UAB coach was well known to most of our fans. UAB was coached by Watson Brown, the older brother of UNC coach Mack Brown. Watson Brown had been an assistant coach at East Carolina for two years under Pat Dye. He was well-respected in the coaching world where ECU played.

The previous year the Pirates and Blazers had played for the first time ever. It was an easy 26-7 ECU win. The expectations in 1999 were for a similar and probably more one-sided victory. The Blazers were 3-5 coming into the game, while the Pirates were 7-1 with wins over nationally ranked Miami and strong wins over West Virginia and South Carolina. The only loss was to a very good Southern Miss team. The Pirates came to Birmingham ranked No. 17 in the polls. The game started as you would expect, as the Pirates took a 17-3 lead late in the first half. An ECU mistake gave the Blazers an easy touchdown, but the Pirates still led 17-10. During the second quarter, UAB defensive back Rodregis Brooks suffered what appeared to be a serious neck injury. He was taken off the field on a stretcher and transported immediately to the hospital. Brooks returned to the field in the third quarter with a 59-yard punt return that set up a touchdown. Then in the fourth quarter, when it looked like the Pirates were going to score, Brooks intercepted an ECU pass and returned it 91 yards for a touchdown. After the second quarter 17-3 lead, the Pirates never scored again and lost 36-17. It was UAB's first win ever over a ranked team and a devastating loss for ECU.

Over the course of the next five games with UAB the Pirates played well at home, winning two out of three but losing both games on the road in mostly empty Legion Field. When 2008 rolled around, except for a win at Samford in the '60s in the pre D1-A FBS era, the Pirates were 0-for-Alabama. This included losses at Alabama, Auburn, three losses at UAB, two bowl losses in Mobile and a loss in the Birmingham Bowl. That's eight losses. Our fans started to think that there was something strange about the state of Alabama.

On a cold night in November, the Pirates played great defense. As was typical of the Holtz era, the Pirates scored just enough to win. ECU had to overcome five turnovers that included three lost fumbles, and the Pirate offense could only muster 56 yards rushing. With just over two minutes remaining in the game, a 2-yard run by Brandon Simmons gave ECU a 17-13 lead. A late interception by Pierre Bell sealed the win, and the long losing streak in Alabama was over.

The rest of the UAB series was all ECU. The next five games were all Pirate victories, finishing with a 63-14 blowout in Greenville that ended the series. When the Pirates moved on to the American Athletic Conference, UAB stayed in Conference USA. At the end of the 2014 season the UAB president announced that due to financial concerns they were shutting down the football program. Part of this was political and had come from a push for a new stadium. For two seasons in 2015 and 2016, the Blazers did not play football. In the meantime they raised the money to start the program again in 2017, and then the most successful season in UAB history came in 2018. They won the division title and then won the Conference USA championship game. They ended the season with a bowl victory over Northern Illinois and finished the year at 11-3. UAB was back from extinction. In the shortened 2020 season, the Blazers again won the Conference USA championship.

In October 2021, the American Athletic Conference announced that UAB would be joining the conference. Although Birmingham is not a major city, it does add a large public university with a well-respected medical center in the football crazy state of Alabama.

The good news kept coming for the Blazers. A city-owned stadium opened in 2021 and became the new home of UAB football. The construction cost was more than $175 million. For the 2022 season, Protective Stadium and Legion Field were the homes for all USFL games, except the playoffs. The stadiums and the City of Birmingham got maximum exposure by hosting all those games.

Carl Davis

University of Alabama

How does a team score three touchdowns and a field goal while the opposing team scores only three touchdowns and still loses by one point? The answer is to play the Alabama Crimson Tide at home.

The one and only time the Pirates have played Alabama was in October 1998 in the middle of a mediocre 6-5 season. In 1998, this was not the Tide of today, but a team that still had a tremendous history, a team that could fill any stadium, and a team that had recruited some high-quality blue-chip athletes.

The 1998 Alabama Crimson Tide was coached by Mike DuBose. They were fifteen years removed from Bear Bryant and his six national championships. The predecessor to DuBose had been Bear Bryant disciple and former assistant Gene Stallings, who won his own national championship at Alabama. The majority of the 1998 team had been recruited by Stallings. They would finish the year with an unremarkable record of 7-5 and a loss in the Music City Bowl.

Our first clue that Alabama was something special was when we arrived at the hotel. There were large arches of red and white balloons everywhere. We finally learned that our ECU travel company had booked our fans into the Alabama team

147

hotel. It became even more obvious when three TV stations set up in front of the hotel to cover the arrival of the home team live on Friday afternoon. There were interviews with Coach DuBose, and the team seemed to almost march through the lobby. We noticed that on each floor of the hotel that housed any players, there was a desk set up in front of the elevator doors. Later that night we saw deputies stationed at each desk, keeping the football players in and others out. Alabama in 1998 was something different.

The game was played at Legion Field in Birmingham, about forty-five minutes from the Alabama campus. This was our first of many trips to Legion Field. The stadium was built in 1927 and although it's been modified many times, it looked worn on that day. Alabama split their home games between Legion Field and Bryant-Denny Stadium in Tuscaloosa. After Bryant-Denny Stadium was expanded and Legion Field was allowed to fall into further disrepair, they moved all their games to campus after 2003. Legion Field did offer a large parking area for RVs, so we had the experience of walking through the RV army. It was a spectacle of flags and food and diehard fans. We were never taunted, but we were not welcomed either. Maybe they were surprised that anyone was willing to walk through enemy territory. Maybe we didn't know any better.

The traveling Alabama RV group is legendary. They generally arrive on Wednesday for the Saturday game. They bring all their supplies with them so that they don't have to spend any money in "enemy territory." One season in the early 2000s is chronicled in the book Rammer Jammer Yellow Hammer by Warren St. John. The author buys an old RV and follows the Crimson Nation for an entire season. One reviewer called it a hilarious travel story and a cultural anthropology of fans. St. John tells the story of the most extreme fans from the most extreme fan base. It's a very good book. He reported that during a TV interview with an Alabama couple, they were asked about the most important thing that they had missed in all the years of following the Crimson Tide. They thought for just a second and answered, "I guess it was our daughter's wedding, but we did get there for the reception. Everyone knows that Alabama plays Tennessee on the third weekend in October."

The game was played in front of more than 80,000 mostly red-clad fans. The Pirates played the first half very conservatively on offense, and Alabama scored three touchdowns to take a 21-0 lead at halftime. Most fans thought the game was over until midway through the third quarter, when receiver Arnie Powell ran a trick play and threw a perfect 35-yard pass to a wide-open Lamont Chappell in the endzone. Then came the most important and most controversial play of the game. The extra point attempt was blocked by Alabama and picked up by a tight end. He lateralled to another player who was trailing the play. The ECU defender seemed to have the angle and went for his legs. It appeared to those of us who were close to the field and within a few yards of the play that he clearly stepped out of bounds. Those who were there that day continue to believe that he stepped out. We were closer and had a better view than the trailing official. The only angle available in video today is from behind, but it seems to show the runner stepping beyond the sideline. I am very confident that with today's video replay, he would have been judged to have been out of bounds. That made the score 23-6 in favor of Alabama.

Later in the third quarter the Pirates got two more touchdowns. The first was a 45-yard pass play and the second was a 43-yard interception return. While the extra point on the first touchdown was successful, the second attempt missed, making the margin 23-19 in favor of the Tide. Early in the fourth quarter the Pirates pulled within a single point on a 36-yard Andrew Bayes field goal. With about five minutes to play on fourth down, the Pirates lined up for a punt. Alabama had thirteen or fourteen players on the field and called a timeout. The issue was that they had used all their timeouts and this was their fourth one in the second half. The officials stopped the clock, the players came off the field, and they restarted the clock. A penalty for calling a timeout, that Alabama didn't have, would have given the Pirates new life and a first down. That's how it ended 23-22 Bama.

The Pirates did get a letter of apology from the SEC officials for the mistake with the timeouts, and most of the Alabama fans that day knew that they had been outplayed. Later that night in a busy restaurant I was standing in the bar trying to get a drink. The mostly Alabama crowd was three-deep at the bar. An Alabama fan saw my ECU shirt and said, "Sir, step up here. You guys deserved to win today!" I will never forget that moment. I will also never forget the freshman quarterback who got the start that day. His name was David Garrard.

Texas Christian University (TCU)

TCU has a lot in common with SMU. Not only are they only forty miles apart and in the same market, they are both private schools with a religious background. Except for four years, they have played every year for more than a century. They share the same background in the old Southwest Conference. TCU was a member of Conference USA for only four years and the Pirates played them twice during those years. They moved on to the Mountain West, and more recently to the Big 12.

Our first encounter with TCU was the inaugural GMAC Bowl in Mobile. Our fans were excited about the game because it was our first bowl in four years and we were playing a good TCU team coached by Dennis Franchione. He was a turnaround artist who left TCU after three years to become the head coach at Alabama and later Texas A&M.

The Horned Frogs were led by LaDainian Tomlinson at running back. He went on to have a great career in the NFL, with more than 1,000 yards in eight consecutive seasons. In the game, Tomlinson had more than 100 yards and ECU had -16 yards on the ground. Our fate was sealed in the fourth quarter when David Garrard's pass was intercepted and returned for a touchdown. TCU won 28-14 in a physical game that they really controlled from the second quarter to the end. Not many games are won when a team has negative rushing yardage.

The Franchione era gave way to the Gary Patterson era in 2001. This was TCU's first year in Conference USA and the one and only time East Carolina has played in Amon G. Carter Stadium on the TCU campus. Patterson had been the defensive coordinator and remained the head coach for twenty-one years until the 2021 season. The Pirates won the game in Fort Worth 37-30.

The stadium was built in 1930, and when ECU played there in 2001 it was not very impressive. In 2010 they did a $105 million renovation and shortly thereafter joined the Big 12 Conference. TCU has had success in the Big 12. Three seasons have produced ten or more wins, and one year they had a conference championship and a 12-1 record. They came within three points of a perfect season. The Big 12 move has been a large step forward for TCU. They really left their longtime rival and former Southwest Conference foe, SMU, well behind.

The game in 2002 in Greenville was noteworthy for a number of reasons. TCU came in ranked No. 22 in the nation with only one loss and an eight-game winning streak. A win in Greenville would give the Conference USA championship to TCU. The Pirates played well, especially on defense where they created seven turnovers. An 81-yard fumble recovery for a touchdown by Travis Heath was the difference in the game.

The win in 2002 over a ranked TCU team was by far the only highlight of an otherwise dismal year for the Pirates. ECU would lose the next two games to Southern Miss and Cincinnati, and Steve Logan would be fired after a 4-8 season.

Incidentally, the TCU mascot, "Horned Frog," is not a frog. It is actually a lizard. The mascot was named in 1897 when the staff of the yearbook noticed that there were lots of these "frogs" on the field where they had just started playing football the year before. Lizards probably wouldn't make such a great mascot name.

My TCU Travel Log:

Visited the Stockyards in Fort Worth and watched the daily cattle drive

PIRATES
vs
USF

SATURDAY
OCT. 26, 2019
HOMECOMING
PAINT IT PURPLE

University of South Florida (USF)

Like the University of Houston, USF is another school in a major city with lots of competition from professional sports teams. While the NBA isn't in Tampa, the USF Bulls compete for fans with the NFL, Major League Baseball, and the NHL. Like Houston, USF is in a college-football-crazy state with very strong high school football programs from which to draw recruits.

While South Florida shares the same type of pro sports competition and is in a state with a strong football culture, that's where the similarity ends. USF is a relative newcomer to college football. They played their first game in 1997, sixty-five years after East Carolina began football. Their first team meeting was held under a tree, and until 2009 the football offices were housed in trailers. The other major difference from most college teams is that USF plays in the 65,000-seat Raymond James Stadium, home of the Tampa Bay Buccaneers. The colors are wrong for South Florida and the stadium has an obvious pirate motif. I have always wanted them to fire the cannons on the huge pirate ship in the endzone when ECU scores! Guess that is not going to happen.

USF is really a mixed bag. They have no real history and play in a pro stadium that is seldom half-full and located more than ten miles from campus, but they play in an area with great interest in football that is also a recruiting hotbed.

South Florida started in Division 1-AA and quickly moved up to 1-A. They joined Conference USA in 2003, but ECU played them in Greenville for the first time a year earlier in 2002. Most East Carolina football fans thought this would be an easy win because of the lack of history and other USF disadvantages, but instead it was a 46-30 loss by the Pirates in a very forgettable 2002 season. It became obvious in that game that USF played hard-nosed physical football. The team seemed to take on the personality of their coach, Jim Leavitt. Their Florida recruits fit his scheme very well.

The Bulls' first trip to Greenville as a member of Conference USA ended with the same result as the previous year, but with a lot more excitement. A 1-8 ECU team played two overtimes with the 6-2 South Florida Bulls. Pirate fullback Vonta Leach scored the tying touchdown with just twenty-one seconds remaining in the game. The teams traded field goals in the first overtime, and both scored touchdowns in the second overtime. ECU lost when Cameron Broadwell's extra point was blocked, giving the victory to USF 38-37. Other than a six-point win at Army, this would be as close as the Pirates would come to a second win in 2003.

2004 saw another lopsided USF 41-17 win, and in 2005 the Bulls moved into the Big East and no longer faced the Pirates. This didn't last long, because both teams had good seasons in 2006 and met again in the first-ever PapaJohns.com Bowl played on Birmingham's Legion Field. ECU was no stranger to old Legion Field, having played Alabama once and UAB three times there, most recently earlier in that same 2006 season. It was not a lucky field. ECU had lost all four previous visits to Legion Field, and that trend didn't change that day. In a made-for-TV game where both groups of fans were forced to sit on the same side of the stadium to make the crowd look larger, the Bulls' quick defense dominated the game. The Bulls won the game 24-7 and finished with a 9-4 record. Coach Jim Leavitt called it the best team in the short history of the University of South Florida. The crowd still looked small on TV, and the Pirates lost and didn't even get pizza. Incredibly, there was no pizza available at Legion Field at the PapaJohns.com Bowl.

In 2007 after the PapaJohns.com Bowl, the Bulls started the season with a quick rise in the polls. They defeated Auburn to start the year and later knocked off No. 5 West Virginia. After six impressive wins, USF was ranked No. 2 in the AP poll. This was quite an accomplishment after such a short history of D-1 football, but then they came crashing back to earth as they lost the next three games in a row.

The Pirates' first win against South Florida came in October 2014 in Tampa. This was the first meeting of the two teams since both had become members of the American Athletic Conference. The Pirates were ranked No. 19 in the country and trailed 17-7 before scoring the next 21 unanswered points. The ECU defense played well, and it was a total team win. Unfortunately for the Pirates, the next five years were very disappointing when it came to games with USF. The Bulls would mostly dominate the Pirates physically and win all five games. The tide would turn in the Covid year of 2020, when the Bulls were down and the Pirates were on the rise. ECU would win the next three years in easy fashion. The most recent game in 2022 was typical of how things had changed. The Pirates coasted to a 48-28 victory. The University of South Florida has come a long way since that first meeting under a tree.

My USF Travel Log:

Enjoyed dining at the Columbia Restaurant in the Ybor City neighborhood of Tampa

Rice University

Rice is a small private research university located in Houston. The Rice and Houston campuses are less than five miles apart, but they are worlds apart with the difference between small private schools and large public universities. Football success has not been a staple at Rice, even with a long history in the Southwest Conference and in a football-centric state like Texas. Like several other schools, when Rice joined Conference USA, the expectation was that the Pirates would likely regularly win easily over the Owls.

The first game was played in Greenville in 2005 shortly after Rice joined the conference. The Pirates came into the game in Skip Holtz's first season 1-3 and had no problem with the Owls. The final score was 41-28.

The next season was ECU's first trip to Rice. The game was played in Rice Stadium, an historic venue built in 1950 that was also the site of Super Bowl VIII. While the stadium originally seated 70,000, tarps covered the endzones and reduced capacity to 47,000. Fewer than 13,000 fans attended the game. Although both teams had lost only two games by later in the season, the Pirates were favored on this trip. The Pirate offense was anything but explosive in spite of the presence of Chris

Johnson, as ECU's 242 rushing yards were overshadowed by only 83 yards in the air. While the Pirates would total 301 yards, Rice would run and pass for 458 yards.

The game began with both teams missing field goals, but then ECU put together a touchdown drive. By halftime, the score was 10-7 in favor of the Pirates. In the third quarter, an ECU possession starting at the one- yard line turned disastrous when a holding penalty in the endzone resulted in a safety. In the fourth quarter with the Pirates leading by eight points, Rice drove 54 yards for a touchdown with only 2:38 remaining. The two-point conversion failed, but then the Pirates went three-and-out and gave the ball back to the Owls. Starting deep in their own territory, Rice moved down the field and kicked the winning field goal with :03 left in the game to win 18-17.

In the final season of the Skip Holtz era, Rice visited Dowdy-Ficklen Stadium. The Pirates controlled and dominated the game 49-13. The following season when the Pirates returned to Houston and Rice Stadium with new coach Ruffin McNeill, it was a Rice blowout. The Owls led in almost every category. Notably, Rice ran for 435 yards against the Pirate defense. The final score was 62-38. The Rice band pretends to be the Stanford band. At this game, they had strings, accordions, and kazoos. They did a Harry Potter show and were all dressed as characters from Harry Potter. After the game in Rice Village, several students we talked to said that they were not aware that Rice played football. They were serious.

In four games while both teams were in Conference USA, ECU and Rice split two and two. Each team won on their home field. There are probably more games in the future, since Rice is coming soon to the American Athletic Conference. Hope they bring the band.

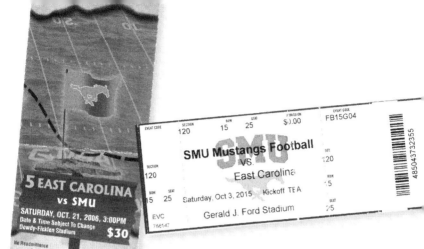

Southern Methodist University (SMU)

Southern Methodist is a school with a rich football history, but also a checkered past. The program was once one of the best in the country and was the pride of Dallas, but to date, SMU is the only school to have received the death penalty for multiple repeated violations of NCAA rules. This happened over the course of many years, but primarily in the '80s. It took decades for SMU to recover; in fact, some would argue that even three decades later parts of the scandal still linger.

Over the years people have asked me about the best game, best stadium, best fans and other "bests." SMU has the best campus when it comes to beauty. Lots of college campuses are crammed into an urban environment, and most of them are landlocked. Many state universities are a crazy mix of architectural styles. It's often the 1940s next door to the 1990s across the street from the 1970s. That is not the case at SMU.

First of all, to get the complete picture of the SMU style you have to consider the neighborhood where the school is located. SMU is in Highland Park, Texas, but the address is Dallas. The town of less than 9,000 adjoins the city, but it is separate. The average per family income there is over $200,000. Many of the wealthiest people in Texas live in that neighborhood. Folks like Dallas Cowboys owner Jerry Jones and former president George Bush are all Highland Park residents and live close to SMU. Laura Bush is an alumna of Southern Methodist, and the George W. Bush Presidential Library is located on campus about two blocks from the football stadium.

The entrance to campus on Bishop Boulevard is just stunning. The main drive is a divided street with a grass median between the lanes. There are huge trees covering both sides of the street, forming a canopy that covers the entire street. They have placed tables all along the center median, and on game day they place red and blue umbrellas in the tables for tailgating. It is a unique scene.

Although it is a small campus, there are broad green lawns in front of each building. The buildings on campus are all red brick and most have white columns. It is extremely well-kept. The football facility is the same. It is all brick and while it is small, it has a nice polished look. It's Gerald Ford Stadium but not THAT Gerald Ford. They have to explain it often.

In 2005 on our first trip to SMU, we participated in a tailgate for ECU fans in front of the SMU law school. It was a warm day and a long walk back toward the stadium, and as we started a young man offered us a ride in a golf cart. We gladly accepted. As we moved through the campus, he gave us a tour. He told us that one building was going to be torn down and replaced with a parking garage, and it looked better than 90 percent of the buildings on most college campuses. Years later we used that parking garage, and it looked just like all the other beautiful campus buildings.

The money and the buildings are impressive, but the football legacy is still there. Many people do not realize the legacy and the history of Southern Methodist football. They played in the Rose Bowl and won a national championship in the late 1930s. SMU played in the Southwestern Conference and won numerous conference championships. They had many great coaches and players. The early 1980s were great for SMU. They had the highest winning percentage of any Division 1 school while playing in a tough conference, but in 1987 it all came crashing down. The Mustangs were on probation starting in 1985 for recruiting violations, but then came the death penalty. It seems that cash had been flowing to players since the early 1970s and some coaches and administrators had known since 1981. The program was shuttered for two years—the first year by the NCAA and the second year voluntarily by SMU.

Things have never really been the same since then. ECU did not encounter the Mustangs until eighteen years after the death penalty. In fact, SMU did not record their second winning season until 2009, twenty-two years after the scandal.

The first two years in the ECU-versus-SMU series were in Conference USA and early in the Skip Holtz era. The Pirates won both games, home and away, rather easily. The next two games were won by SMU in 2009 and 2010. The 2009 SMU team was the best team in a generation and finished 8-5 with a win in the Sheraton Hawaii Bowl. They had managed to hire former NFL and Hawaii coach June Jones to come to Dallas. ECU was favored in that game, but it just didn't happen on defense and special teams. The first SMU touchdown came on a blocked field goal attempt that was returned for 63 yards. The second SMU touchdown came on a 96-yard touchdown pass that tied an SMU school record. In spite of ECU controlling most of the game, those two plays made it 28-21.

The next year the two teams played to a draw in Greenville. In fact, there was only a two-yard difference in the total yardage for the game. With the score tied at 38, the Pirates won the toss in overtime and chose defense. SMU scored, but the Pirates lost when Dominick Davis had his pass picked off. The final score was 45-38. That was the end of the Conference USA era between the two teams.

SMU joined the American Athletic Conference one year before ECU in 2013. They had made overtures toward the Big 12 as a possible replacement for Texas A&M, but were skipped over for their rivals TCU and West Virginia. East Carolina's first game in the AAC was against SMU in October 2014, and it was Homecoming. The game came two weeks after the Pirates had pounded UNC 70-41, so the crowd was pumped up for the game. ECU was ranked No. 22 and had a 4-1 record. Quarterback Shane Carden did not disappoint the fans, throwing for more than 400 yards and replacing David Garrard with the most career passing yards in ECU history. The Pirates rolled to an easy victory 45-21. SMU would win their last game of the year against UConn and finish 1-11 to end the June Jones era in Dallas.

The next two seasons were mirror images of each other. In 2015 on the road, ECU had an easy win 49-23. At home in Greenville in 2016, the Pirates were no match for SMU and lost 55-31. The Pirates and Mustangs would split the next two games as well. SMU still seems to struggle with the death penalty legacy and now is in the shadow of the successful TCU program thirty-five miles away. ECU and SMU will never be rivals. They both love football but are very different institutions and are 1,300 miles apart.

My SMU Travel Log:

Visited the sixth floor of the Texas School Book Depository and Dealey Plaza

Ate dinner at the Egyptian restaurant where Jack Ruby ate the night before he shot Lee Harvey Oswald

Navy (USNA)

The atmosphere at Navy is similar to the atmosphere at Army. The Midshipmen parade in groups into the stadium and fill the field. They stand for the entire game. They cheer and sing as a complete unit. The stadium is a few blocks off campus and relatively close to the scenic docks, with beautiful ships everywhere. While the stadium is not as old as the facility at Army, it has the look of tradition. In the ring below the upper deck, where most schools list championships, bowls or great players, Navy lists great naval battles. These include battles like Guadalcanal, Midway and Iwo Jima. My best friend described it perfectly when he said, "These guys play a helluva schedule."

Although Navy is a service academy like Army, the two programs are very different. There are multiple reasons, but starting in 2002 it was all about coaching. With the hiring of Paul Johnson and later Ken Niumatalolo, the Midshipmen put together a very impressive run, not just for a service academy, but for any program.

The problem shared by the service academies is one of recruiting. Since the players have to be students and later military officers, it takes a very special pitch to find the right athletes. Marginal students are just not admitted, no matter how good they may be on the field. Generally, those recruits do not have the dream of playing in the NFL since they are committed to the service upon graduation. Very few have become NFL players—with Roger Staubach being a notable exception, but in a very different era. He was the last player from a military academy to win a Heisman trophy.

Coach Johnson seized upon an offense that worked for a disciplined team, the option. The Navy team learned by repetition and executed it perfectly, game after game and year after year. Coach Ken Niumatalolo followed Johnson and continued with the same successful scheme. Navy has had a winning record in fifteen of the last nineteen seasons.

Most football fans know that the success of the option is based on the difficulty in defending it. The defense must be disciplined. They have to follow their assigned man and not follow the ball. It's hard to do when your entire life playing football you have always "gone to the ball." The other difficulty is the fact that so few teams run this offense, so you only see it against Navy. The defense practices all spring and fall but usually only gets deep into studying the option the week before the game. If you don't think that Navy and the option have been effective against ECU, three of the four games where the Pirates have yielded the most rushing yards in our history were against Navy, and all since 2010. It was 521 yards in 2010, 512 yards in 2012 and 480 yards yielded in 2016. 2015 didn't make the top five, but the Pirates gave up 415 rushing yards to Navy that year. Needless to say, few teams give up that kind of yardage and win the game, and the Pirates lost all four. In the 2010 loss, ECU gave up 76 points, the second most in program history and the most since the first ECU home game in 1932. In five games Navy has never lost in Dowdy-Ficklen stadium.

East Carolina has had four close games with Navy and come away with two wins, both by three points, and two losses by three and five points. In the loss in 2006, the defense held Navy to only 28 points. The Greg Hudson defense still yielded 403 yards on the ground. In the first win, 38-35, the Pirates held the Midshipmen to less than 300 yards on the ground, but it still took a record-setting performance by Dominique Davis to secure the win. Davis completed the first twenty-six passes that he threw. The second win was also 38-35 in 2021 on the road in Annapolis. This game ended with a walkoff field goal by Owen Daffer as time expired. The most recent close loss came in 2022. The Pirate defense held the Midshipmen to only 17 points and less than 200 yards rushing. Unfortunately, the Pirate offense never got any rhythm and could only score 17 points in regulation. The hero of the 2021 game, Owen Daffer, was wide left on a field goal attempt that would have forced a third overtime. Navy won yet another close game 23-20 in two overtimes to make it five wins in a row in Greenville.

My Navy Travel Log:

Walked the downtown area of Annapolis around the docks

Toured the Naval Academy

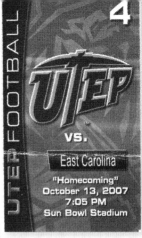

The University of Texas El Paso (UTEP)

UTEP is a unique institution and shares a number of things in common with ECU. The most notable is that both schools are somewhat isolated from other parts of their state and serve as a hub for the region. This is true in education, medicine, and football. West Texas is a football-obsessed area, and UTEP is no exception. There is also a similar blue collar ethic. It's true that the two schools were never considered rivals in Conference USA, but there was mutual respect.

Many people think of UTEP as a basketball school. They won a national championship as Texas Western over an outstanding Kentucky team. Their team was all-black and Kentucky's was all-white. Texas Western was the first school in the South to integrate athletics, and it was a huge upset on a national stage.

UTEP was founded as the State School for Mining and Metallurgy. The mascot is a miner and the cultural influences of mining and the city's proximity to Mexico still prevail.

The Miners play in the Sun Bowl Stadium with more than 51,000 seats. It is simply a beautiful football environment, one of the best natural settings in all of college football. The stadium is truly a bowl carved into the top of a mountain. The sun setting on the mountains beyond the stadium is spectacular. The stadium is obviously also home of the annual Sun Bowl game.

The Pirates are 3-1 overall against the Miners. The first game in 2007 was by far the most exciting. Unfortunately, many fans on the East Coast didn't get to see it due to the time difference and the late start. The game began at 9:05pm on the East Coast and ended just before 1 a.m. This football game had it all. In the first quarter, Van Eskridge had a 50-yard fumble return for a touchdown. Late in the second quarter UTEP put together a 40-plus yard drive in 24 seconds and kicked a field goal to take a 19-18 lead. In the third quarter, a 50-yard receiver reverse by Dwayne Harris and a 80-yard pass play thrown by Dwayne Harris gave the Pirates the lead going into the fourth. On the first play of the fourth quarter, the Miners scored a touchdown to tie the game. The rest of the quarter was a draw, until what looked like the winning drive in the last two minutes by UTEP. A 31-yard run with 34 seconds remaining in the game gave the Miners a 7-point lead. ECU quarterback Rob Kass started 71 yards from the goal and used the clock perfectly. As time expired, Kass threw a perfect 33-yard bullet to Juwon Crowell standing at the 1-yard line. He caught the ball, turned and stepped into the endzone. After the extra point, we headed to overtime tied at 39. The Pirate defense held the Miners to a 45-yard field goal and then Rob Kass directed a 25-yard drive ending with his own 1-yard run to win an unbelievable game 45-42.

The teams met the following year in Greenville and the Pirates won very easily, 53-21. ECU returned to El Paso in 2011, this time with the Air Raid offense, but the Pirates could only manage 133 yards passing. It was a low scoring game, with UTEP taking a 5-point lead in the middle of the fourth quarter. After a big defensive stop, the Pirates had time for a winning drive. Unlike the last visit to El Paso, there was no magic and Dominique Davis was intercepted, effectively ending the game.

The final time the teams played was the next year in 2012 in Greenville. It was a memorable game, but more for the weather than for the action on the field. There was an eighty minute rain and lightning delay in the first half. Then there was a shortened halftime and more rain. In spite of the weather, the Pirates had 475 yards of offense. UTEP got a late score, but it was essentially all Pirates 28-18.

Needless to say, distance has prevented this from ever being a rivalry. It's a 3,800 mile round trip to UTEP. This was the most distant conference opponent in ECU history. UTEP has an excellent football culture and it is truly a beautiful football setting, but it is a long way from Eastern North Carolina.

My UTEP Travel Log:

Took side trips to Carlsbad Caverns and White Sands

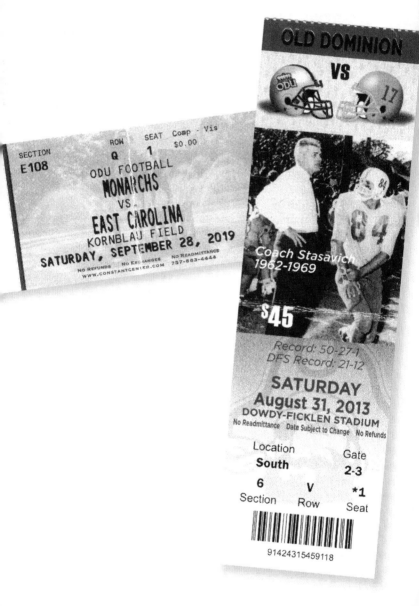

Old Dominion University (ODU)

Old Dominion is geographically our closest out-of-state rival. The school started out as a part of William & Mary, only becoming truly separate in 1962. With a smaller enrollment and an urban environment, there is not a direct comparison between the two other than the fact that we both draw students from northeastern North Carolina.

The football program began almost immediately after the school was established in the early 1930s but was discontinued after only eleven years. After many years without football on the ODU campus, the program was restarted in 2009—the result of many alumni and administrators wanting to provide a better experience for the students and the community. Old Dominion started play as an independent in Division 1 as an independent in FCS. In the Monarchs' recent short football history they have been an independent and the member of three different conferences. They were a member of the Colonial Athletic Conference (CAA) for only two years and stepped up to the FBS level and joined Conference USA in 2013. During the conference realignment and beginning with the 2022 season, the Monarchs left Conference USA to join the expanding Sun Belt Conference.

The Pirates have faced Old Dominion four times in their brief football history beginning in 2013, which would be their final season as a FCS team. It was the season opener in Greenville and Shane Carden had a good day, throwing 46 completions for 447 yards and five Pirate touchdowns. It was a close first half, with ODU scoring three times. The Pirates led 21-17. Early in the fourth quarter ECU finally gained some separation and won by a final score of 52-38. The Pirate faithful had not expected such a close game, but they learned about future NFL quarterback Taylor Heinicke. He had 338 passing yards and three touchdowns in a losing effort.

The next meeting was also in Greenville. It would come five years later in Scottie Montgomery's final season with the Pirates. Again this would be another story of the Pirates getting more yardage, but scoring did not come easy. The Pirates only led 21-20 at the half and were down one score late in the fourth quarter until Reid Herring, one of the three quarterbacks used by the PIrates that day, hit Tahj Dean with a short pass to bring ECU within one point. The extra point would be blocked so the Pirates would hold the Monarchs and get the ball back, and then Jake Verity would kick the winning field goal with 46 seconds remaining to seal the victory 37-35. Again, like five years earlier, this was not what Pirate Nation expected playing Old Dominion.

The two teams would play again the very next season. This time the game was played in Norfolk at S.B. Ballard Stadium, formerly Foreman Field. This venue was constructed in 1936. After Old Dominion abandoned football it was used for multiple purposes, including the playing of the annual Oyster Bowl. It went through multiple renovations until finally it could no longer meet the building codes and was torn down and completely rebuilt. The Pirates, under first-year head coach Mike Houston, would travel there on that first season after the construction. While the stadium is small, only seating just over 22,000, it looked modern and was full of Monarchs and traveling Pirates. Early on it appeared the Pirates might run away with the game. They led 17-3 at the half. The teams were evenly matched, with each creating three turnovers and having almost identical total yardage. Holton Ahlers would throw two touchdown passes. The Monarchs would make it close by scoring on a long 88-yard drive with just over two minutes remaining in the game. The Pirates would recover the onsides kick and escape Norfolk with a 24-21 win.

The fourth game in the series came on a rainy night in Greenville three years later. Holton Ahlers again threw two touchdown passes for ECU. The difference this time would be the Pirate running game. Keaton Mitchell would rush for 164 yards, including a fourth quarter run for 81 yards and a score. Rahjai Harris and Marlon Gunn would add another 100-plus yards. The game was close until early in the fourth quarter, when Mitchell broke through and scored. On ODU's next play, quarterback Hayden Wolff was stripped of the ball and ECU would recover. Harris would rush for 43 yards and a score, sealing the win. The Pirates wore down the Monarchs, 39-21.

The four games in this series have all gone the way of the Pirates. ECU fans have expected domination. That has not been the case. Two of the four games have been decided by three points. Old Dominion looks like it may become a long-term rival.

On the ticket:

UNDAUNTED

Thursday, October 23, 2014

UCONN
GAME 4
EAST CAROLINA

ACCT | GATE | PRICE
12580 | 2-3 | $54.0
SEC | ROW | SEA
6 | V | *1
Dowdy-Ficklen Stadium
No Admittance Date Subject to Change No R

Paint It Black

University of Connecticut (UConn)

Unfortunately for East Carolina, UConn was never a rival. First of all, UConn was and is and will forever be a basketball school. There is no amount of money from a conference or a donor that will ever change that. The school is rooted in basketball, and that's the culture of UConn and the culture of the region.

In my broadcasting career, my fourteen-year stop at UNC-TV taught me the importance of college sports to public television. The very first program ever broadcast on UNC-TV was a basketball game in 1955 between Wake Forest and UNC-Chapel Hill. While at UNC-TV, I learned that Connecticut Public Television had a similar story years later. In the early 1990s, they began broadcasting UConn women's basketball. The programming people asked the question, "Who is going to watch?" The team went 35-0, and they got their answer. With little competition in sports broadcasting, UConn women's basketball became a large revenue source for Connecticut Public Television. They are the most successful women's basketball program in the nation, with eleven national championships. It was a very big deal when they lost the contract to commercial broadcasters many years later.

The success of UConn basketball with both mens and womens teams did little, if anything, to help UConn football. In his five years there in the late '90s, Skip Holtz was the most successful coach in more than 100 years of UConn football. His winning percentage was .596, so the bar was not too high.

Shortly after the Holtz years, UConn was invited to join the Big East. This was partly a regional thing and mostly a basketball thing. Enthusiasm was really high in 2004 when they entered the Big East and opened a brand-new football stadium, Rentschler Field. The land was donated by the Pratt and Whitney Company, and most of the money was appropriated by the legislature. The State of Connecticut still owns the stadium. The location was chosen because Hartford was trying to entice the New England Patriots to move south to Hartford. When that didn't work, they built a stadium primarily for UConn football. Unfortunately for the university, Rentschler Field is twenty miles west of the campus. As I have seen with other off-campus stadiums, this really hampers the game day experience.

UConn did benefit from membership in the Big East, even in football. The BCS money in those years was a boost to the program. In 2006, they opened a $57 million football center and training complex. They also benefited from competition with Big East schools like Miami, West Virginia, Syracuse, Pittsburgh and Boston College. They became a "charter" member of the AAC in 2013 when the non-FBS schools bought the Big East name and separated.

East Carolina's history with UConn began in the AAC in 2014. The Pirates hold a 4-1 advantage. In three of those games UConn was not competitive. In one game, ECU was very lucky to win. In one game, the Pirates were dominated by a 6-7 UConn team.

In 2015, ECU played at Rentschler Field for the first time. The stadium sits in a large open space outside of the city. The announced crowd of 23,000 was probably half that large. The cold temperatures, lack of a name opponent, mediocre season and general football apathy made for a less-than-exciting atmosphere. The Pirates kept it close for the first half, but quarterback James Summers for most of the game and Blake Kemp in the fourth quarter combined for only 137 yards passing. They threw four interceptions and only scored one offensive touchdown. The Pirates lost 31-13. It was an ugly loss to a mediocre team in front of a small crowd on a cold night.

On the next trip to Hartford in 2017, it was a day game in late September with a temperature in the 80s. The weather was unusually warm for Connecticut that time of year. The Pirates completely dominated, with Duke transfer Thomas Sirk having a great game. He threw for 426 yards and three touchdowns. With eleven minutes remaining in the third period, ECU led 41-21. For the next 26 minutes, the Pirate defense was ineffective. For the entire game, each team gained 596 yards. UConn lined up for the tying field goal with a few seconds remaining. It was wide right, preserving ECU's first win of the season, 41-38. Both teams would finish the season with identical 3-9 records.

As UConn departed the AAC, it was hard to see a future for their football program that is so overshadowed by basketball. Going forward, UConn is not a good candidate for conference membership. They can always fill their schedule with teams looking for an easy win. From an ECU perspective, UConn was not a natural rival, and neither fan base was excited by the prospect of playing the other.

Brigham Young University (BYU)

Brigham Young is a university with a solid and rich football history and tradition with a national profile. That history is mostly built around their legendary coach LeVell Edwards. He was promoted from an assistant to head coach and remained there for twenty-eight years. Edwards only had one losing season during his years at BYU. He was known as an early adopter of the West Coast Offense, and his program was copied by schools and coaches from all over the country. Today, LaVell Edwards Stadium is named in his honor.

BYU has played at the highest level, and the Cougars won a national championship in 1984. They were ranked No. 1 in both the AP and the Coaches Poll. BYU is the last team from a non-power conference to win a national championship. That championship raised the profile of the team and the university. Since 2000, they have played in a bowl game twenty out of the last twenty-one seasons. They continued to develop a national recruiting program and continued to recruit high-quality players. BYU won multiple WAC and Mountain West conference championships before becoming an independent in 2011. That changed their scheduling, but the national profile made them a desirable opponent for any team east of the

Mississippi. They will soon join UCF, Houston and Cincinnati in moving to the Big 12 Conference.

A trip to Provo, Utah and LaVell Edwards Stadium is a unique experience. First of all, the setting for the stadium is in the Utah Valley at almost a mile above sea level. While it sits in a "valley," the mountains are close by and seem to almost tower over the stadium. It creates a beautiful natural bowl. With more than 63,000 seats, BYU does an excellent job of filling them.

The BYU atmosphere for visitors is the most polite you will encounter anywhere. They have "ambassadors"—older gentlemen who wear blue shirts with the school logo and blue ties. They offer to assist you any way they can. We observed an ambassador offering free "Cougar Tails" to parents with children in the visitors section. These are large doughnut-like pastries that are iced in blue. It was a sincere and genuine gesture to make sure that the children enjoyed their experience. The ambassadors always made sure it was alright with the parents before offering the sugary treat!

The most difficult thing for a visitor to do is to visit the restroom! It takes a long time, because you will be repeatedly stopped and asked questions like, "Where is East Carolina?" or "Are you enjoying your stay in Utah?" The rank-and-file Brigham Young fans, as well as the ambassadors, all seem to have a welcoming attitude toward visitors. As most traveling fans know, this is not very common.

East Carolina's first game with BYU came in 2015 in Provo. The Pirates started fast and led 14-7 at the end of the first quarter. When quarterback James Summers and the offense stalled, backup quarterback Blake Kemp rallied the Pirates. Entering the fourth quarter ECU was down 38-21, but then Kemp led three long drives for scores. The Pirates intercepted a pass near midfield with five minutes remaining in the game. Blake Kemp drove the offense to the 16-yard line, where unfortunately the drive stalled and ECU had to settle for a field goal. This tied the score at 38. The Cougars drove the ball on a 10-play, four-minute scoring drive and pushed it into the endzone with 19 seconds left in the game. The final score was 45-38 BYU.

The 2015 season would end with nine wins for BYU, and Coach Bronco Mendenhall would move on after the season to Virginia. 2015 would be Coach Ruffin McNeil's final year as well. He would join Mendenhall at Virginia for the 2016 season as an assistant.

The next meeting with the Cougars would be in 2017 in Greenville for Homecoming. Both the Pirates and the Cougars were having rough seasons. The Pirates were 1-5 and the Cougars were 2-6. The game was tied at 10 at the half. ECU was led by Duke graduate transfer quarterback Thomas Sirk, who was replaced in the second half by backup quarterback Gardner Minshew. He had a productive fourth quarter, throwing two touchdown passes. The Pirates would win easily 33-17.

This would be one of only three wins in 2017 for the Pirates, while BYU only won four games. It was a bad year for both programs and the worst for BYU in almost fifty years.

The Pirates would travel for the second time to Provo in October 2022 for a Friday night game. The teams entered the game heading in opposite directions. The Pirates came to Utah after a big win over UCF and on a two game winning streak. The Cougars were on a three game losing streak after being ranked as high as No. 12 in the nation earlier in the season. The Pirates started slowly on offense and both teams found the endzone and made the score 17-17 at the half. While the first half was about offense, the second half was about defense. Each team scored a touchdown in the third quarter and the Pirates stopped the Cougars on fourth down twice in the fourth quarter. One last ECU drive set up a 33-yard field goal by Andrew Conrad as time expired. The Pirates would win

27-24 on what Coach Houston said "may be the ugliest game-winning field goal in history."

BYU, while operating as an independent, has been able to maintain an excellent revenue stream. ESPN has been helpful for a number of years. This is unusual, but they have become a much sought-after out-of-conference opponent by many schools. The Big 12 will enhance their revenue, and they will likely be very competitive in their new conference starting in 2023.

While it's not a natural rivalry, the longstanding national profile of Brigham Young makes this a good game for East Carolina. With BYU's consistently good football program, they tend to be a measuring stick for the teams that they play.

My BYU Travel Log:

Visited Yellowstone with mountains, lakes, and geysers, where I saw animals of all kinds— including a human who went running across a field with his young son trying to get closer to a pack of wolves.

Conferences

In East Carolina's history, the football program has been a member of four different conferences. The roles of conferences have changed dramatically over the years, changing again in the past few years. ECU's conference membership has never been more important than it is today.

Conference affiliation for East Carolina started in 1947 in the North State Conference. The conference began in 1930 with seven original charter members, all from small North Carolina schools. Western Carolina was added in 1933, and the Pirates became the ninth member in 1947. The name was changed to the Carolinas Conference in 1961. This affiliation provided as many as six scheduling opportunities a year, all within North Carolina.

East Carolina would leave the Carolinas Conference in 1962 and become an independent school and a NCAA Division 1 member. Independence didn't last long. In fact, two years later the Pirates joined the Southern Conference. This conference was founded in 1921 with schools like the University of Alabama, the University of Tennessee, North Carolina and North Carolina State. Those schools and many others left to form the Southeastern Conference and the Atlantic Coast Conference. In the mid-1930s, they would be replaced by

smaller schools from North and South Carolina, Virginia, and West Virginia. The Pirates would remain a member of the Southern Conference for the next thirteen years. During that time, they would win the conference championship four times under three different coaches.

The Pirates left the Southern Conference at the end of the 1976 season. They would claim the conference championship in that final year under Coach Pat Dye. Once again East Carolina had become an independent. One year later in 1978, the NCAA would divide Division 1 schools into 1-A and 1-AA. East Carolina became 1-A, with the larger schools leaving behind the former members of the Southern Conference in Division 1-AA. This was an important step in the progress of ECU football.

For the next twenty years East Carolina was an independent in college football. Schedules for the first few years of independence were a mix of old former Southern Conference competitors and new teams in Division 1-A. By the mid '80s the Pirates were playing predominantly more notable schools like Virginia Tech, Illinois, Florida State and Miami, along with the Division 1-A schools in North Carolina. Schedules consisted of eleven games per season, and the Pirates struggled to schedule name opponents in Greenville. Many larger schools wanted two-for-one games, or even three-or-four--to-one games, to get home games for the Pirates. For the seasons 1989 through 1999, East Carolina only played five home games each season in Dowdy-Ficklen Stadium. There were a few neutral site games, but it was a distinct scheduling disadvantage being an independent at ECU.

In 1997 East Carolina became a football member of Conference USA. This was the first time in twenty years that ECU had been a conference member. Unlike the previous conference affiliations, the members of C-USA were much larger schools, and Conference USA was not a regional conference. The Pirates' closest conference competitor would be Louisville, more than 600 miles away. The most distant would be UTEP, more than 1,900 miles away in the Mountain Time Zone. While Conference USA offered more money to each school, the travel was extensive. This was important because ECU became a full member in all sports in 2000. For the previous nineteen years, the Pirates had been a member of the Colonial Athletic Association for sports other than football. The CAA was made up of schools in the region that either didn't have a football program, like UNC-Wilmington, or played in Division 1-AA, like James Madison. Because of the Pirates' success in the '90s, coming into Conference USA many Pirate fans were expecting ECU to dominate and compete for the conference championship. This didn't happen. The Pirates consistently won within the conference but never reached the conference championship game for eleven seasons. Finally the Skip-Holtz-led Pirates played for and won the conference championship in 2008 and 2009.

The move to the relatively new American Athletic Conference happened for East Carolina in 2014 after an extensive lobbying campaign by Athletic Director Terry Holland and other campus leaders. The AAC was formed as part of a reorganization of the Big East Conference in the previous year. The football-playing Big East members became AAC members, and the non-football schools retained the Big East name. Several of the football schools had been members of the Big East for several years before the reorganization, most coming from Conference USA. Since the Big East was a "BCS" conference, they shared in the proceeds from the BCS Championship that went to the six BCS conferences. This was a very significant advantage for the teams already in the AAC, who got a big head start on ECU. When the Pirates joined the

American Athletic Conference they were then a part of the "Group of Five."

As things have changed with conferences, so have traditions like college football on Saturday and so has regionalism. There used to be a Thursday night ESPN made-for-television production on the schedule every year or two. It was a big deal, because it attracted a national audience and large stadium crowds. One season East Carolina played on five different days of the week. The following year the Pirates played in four different time zones.

Bowls

The subject of bowls is an interesting one. Bowls have changed as much as anything in college football in the past twenty-five years. A bowl invitation used to be something special for a school and a team. Now it's expected. In fact, a coach that doesn't get his team to a bowl in a few years will be looking for a new job. In 2022 there are forty-one bowl games, including the college football playoff. That means that at least eighty teams will get a bowl invitation and this doesn't count the FCS playoffs. That's well over 60 percent of all the teams playing FBS football. One argument about "too many bowls" is that it is not really a reward for a team. It has become expected. The less prestigious bowls have become less of a big local event for the community sponsoring the bowl. When there were fewer bowls, they included parades, pep rallies, a battle of the bands, elaborate parties, and celebrations. While the Rose Bowl and the events surrounding it like the parade are as big as ever, most other bowl locations have not made these events very special in their communities. Sadly, bowls have become made-for-television events with a payout to each school. In many ways, it is just another away game during the holidays. It does provide a nice reward for the players and coaches and fans, but it's not very special.

In the early years, coaches Jack Boone and Clarence Stasavich took the Pirates to bowl games in 1952 and 1954 and in three consecutive years, 1963, 1964 and 1965. They won all three games under Coach Stas in the '60s.

The first year of the split between Division 1-A and 1-AA saw the 8-3 Pirates under Coach Pat Dye head to Shreveport, La. to play in the Independence Bowl. The local Louisiana Tech team was not a match for the Pirates, and they rolled to a 35-13 victory. It would cap a nine-win season for ECU. The Pirates would not have another season with at least nine wins until thirteen years and three coaches later.

Much has been written and even more has been said about the 1992 Peach Bowl and the magical 1991 season. The circumstances of the comeback, with 20 unanswered points, created a storybook ending. This followed a season with outstanding and memorable players and special endings and considering the opponent, NC State, it is easily one of the most special games in ECU's long football history. It completed ECU's only eleven-win season. The theme of "We Believe" lives on more than 30 years later.

As an independent, East Carolina didn't have any automatic bowl invitations from a conference. This was very limiting with fewer bowls available. In 1994, the Pirates were invited to play in the Liberty Bowl in Memphis. They were matched with the University of Illinois. The Pirates were looking for revenge, because in 1991 the Illini had spoiled ECU's perfect season during the first game of the year on the road, 38-31. Illinois totally dominated the game and did it without scoring in the fourth quarter. They won the game 30-0.

The next year, 1995, the Pirates were again invited to the Liberty Bowl. This time the opponent was Stanford. The Pirates didn't get much respect coming into the game. The Stanford band performed "East Carolina the 51st State" at halftime. It was not complimentary. The game was not a good one for ECU quarterback Marcus Crandell, but the defense would score once and hold on for a 19-13 win.

1999 would be the next bowl game for the Pirates in the inaugural GMAC Bowl in Mobile, AL. TCU was the opponent with future All-American and future Pro Bowler LaDainian Tomlinson. The Pirate defense held Tomlinson to 127 yards rushing, but the ECU offense could only generate two scores. TCU would win the first GMAC Bowl 28-14.

The Pirates were back in a bowl the next year in Houston in the Astrodome. Their opponent would be Texas Tech under new coach Mike Leach, and the Red Raider quarterback would be current Arizona Cardinals coach Kliff Kingsbury. The Pirate running game would lead the way, and an electrifying 71-yard punt return by Keith Stokes would give ECU a 40-14 lead going into the fourth quarter. The GalleryFurniture.com Bowl would end with a Pirate win and a final score of 40-27.

For the third year in a row, East Carolina was back in a bowl game, this time back in Mobile at the GMAC Bowl against Marshall. Although the circumstances were much different, in the 2001 GMAC Bowl, the outcome was the same. After leading 38-8 at the half, Marshall would tie the game with just seven seconds remaining. The Thundering Herd would go on to win 64-61 in double overtime.

It would be five years and two coaches later before the Pirates were invited back to a bowl game. Skip Holtz would take ECU to the PapaJohn's.com Bowl at Legion Field in Birmingham, Alabama. The opponent would be the South Florida Bulls. The Pirates would produce 30 yards more offense than South Florida but lose a game where neither team scored in the 2nd half, 24-7.

The next year East Carolina would travel to Hawaii to face Boise State in the 2007 Sheraton Hawaii Bowl. Many folks have called it the Chris Johnson Bowl. Johnson had a record 408 all-purpose yards. All of that didn't prevent Boise State from tying the game on a field goal with just over one minute to play. Ben Hartman would win the game for the Pirates with a 34-yard field goal. It was an exciting ECU win, 41-38.

As champions of Conference USA, East Carolina would play the University of Kentucky in the Liberty Bowl in January 2009. The Pirates would lead 16-3 at the half, but Kentucky would seize the momentum by returning the opening kickoff of the second half for a touchdown. ECU could only manage a field goal in the second half. A blocked punt by Kentucky that was returned for a touchdown with three minutes left in the game would give the Wildcats the victory, 25-19.

For the fourth year in a row, Skip Holtz led the Pirates to a bowl game. It was back to Memphis and the 2010 Liberty Bowl to meet the Arkansas Razorbacks from the Southeastern Conference. Before the game, the bowl committee had organized a tailgate in an old exhibition building on the fairgrounds next to the stadium. The temperature was just below freezing, and the building had no heat. Afterwards, it was described as the "World's Coldest Indoor Tailgate." ECU dominated in yardage, first downs, and time of possession, but had a hard time scoring on a very cold windy night. In the closing minutes, kicker Ben Hartman missed two field goals, either one of which would have won the game. He would miss another field goal to extend the game to a second overtime and Arkansas would win the game 20-17. It was a bitter loss after dominating the football game.

The Ruffin-McNeill-led Pirates would be invited to the Military Bowl played in RFK Stadium in Washington. The opponent would be Maryland in the final season of Ralph Friedgen's coaching career with Terrapins. The Pirates found it difficult to run the ball and only could manage 32 yards on the ground. Maryland ran the ball at will and put up 51 points as a result. It was a perfect send off for Coach Friedgen, a 51-20 win.

The Pirates would be back in a bowl two years later in New Orleans in the Superdome. They faced the Ragin' Cajuns of the University of Louisiana-Lafayette in the R+L Carriers New Orleans Bowl. While a majority of the crowd of 48,000 were Cajun fans, the Pirates overcame the home field advantage and kept the game within reach. While Shane Carden had a good game, Louisiana's Terrence Broadway had a better game. The Ragin' Cajuns would win by a final score of 43-34.

It was back to a bowl again in 2013 as ECU was invited to play in the Beef 'O' Brady's Bowl at Tropicana Field in St. Petersburg. The opponent would be the Bobcats of Ohio University from the MAC Conference. In the first quarter it was all ECU, as the Pirates led 14-0. But during the second quarter the tables turned and by early in the fourth quarter ECU was trailing 20-17. An almost-200-yard performance, including two fourth quarter touchdowns by Vintavious Cooper, made the difference. It would be the Pirates' first bowl win since the Hawaii Bowl. The final score was 37-20.

The next year, ECU would meet Florida in the 2015 Birmingham Bowl at Legion Field. The Pirates scored first, but the Gators got an interception return and two touchdowns in the second quarter to lead 21-7 at the half. A fumble at the goal line gave Florida the momentum. The teams traded touchdowns and ECU got two field goals but could never draw even. A 400-plus yard performance by Shane Carden was just not enough. Like the 2010 Liberty Bowl, the Pirates outplayed their opponent on offense but had trouble scoring. This time they would lose 28-20.

The 2021 season ended with seven wins and an invitation back to the Military Bowl. The game is now played at Navy Marine Memorial Stadium in Annapolis. Unfortunately the game was canceled when the Boston College Eagles could not play due to a Covid-19 outbreak on the team. There were many questions raised about the number of players who were unable to play versus how many just didn't want to play the game. Lots of disappointed Pirate fans had made the trip to Annapolis by the time the game was canceled.

East Carolina's bowl history is a mixture of some super highs and awful lows. The highs were the 1992 Peach Bowl and the 2007 Sheraton Hawaii Bowl, while the lows were the 2001 GMAC Bowl and the 2010 Autozone Liberty Bowl. What is missing from this history is at least two years when the Pirates should have played in bowl games. There were not as many bowl game opportunities in those years, and the size of the fan base mattered. In 1983, Ed Emory's Pirates team went 8-3, losing by a total of 13 points to Florida, Florida State and Miami. All were ranked teams, and all the games were on the road. Miami was the eventual national champion. In 1983 there were only sixteen bowls, and an 8-3 North Carolina team got a bid to the Peach Bowl while the Pirates stayed home. In 1996, Steve Logan said he knew the Pirates would not go bowling when they lost to Southern Miss. The 1996 team would finish 8-3. The losses besides Southern Miss would be at No. 25 West Virginia and at No. 10 Virginia Tech. By 1996 there were still only eighteen bowl games including the BCS, so competition for bowl slots was fierce.

September 1, 2007 - After a $100,000 donation to the Hokie Hope Fund following the shooting the previous May, the fans and the university showed their appreciation to ECU.

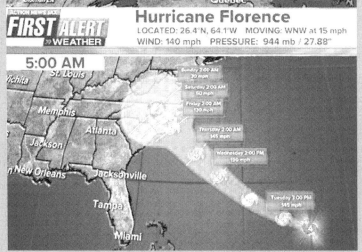

September 12, 2018 - NWS projections for Hurricane Florence early on the morning when ECU canceled the game with VaTech.

Marshall

Marshall campus memorial to the plane crash victims of 1970.

ECU memorial to the 1970
Marshall team located outside
the visitors' locker room at
Dowdy Ficklen Stadium.

Imitation is the sincerest form of flattery.

November 25, 2006 - With time expiring NC State officials stopped the clocked and lowered the goal posts.

Poor Crowds

November 23, 2013 - With the Pirates up 42-14, State fans headed for the exits. State would score twice in the last 0:51 to make it 42-28.

September 28, 2013 - Tar Heels appear to have left the premises late in the fourth quarter of a 55-31 Pirate win.

Southern Miss proudly says that they will play Anyone Anywhere Anytime.

Jolly Roger

The first time the Skull and Crossbones "Jolly Roger" is officially raised at Dowdy Ficklen Stadium.

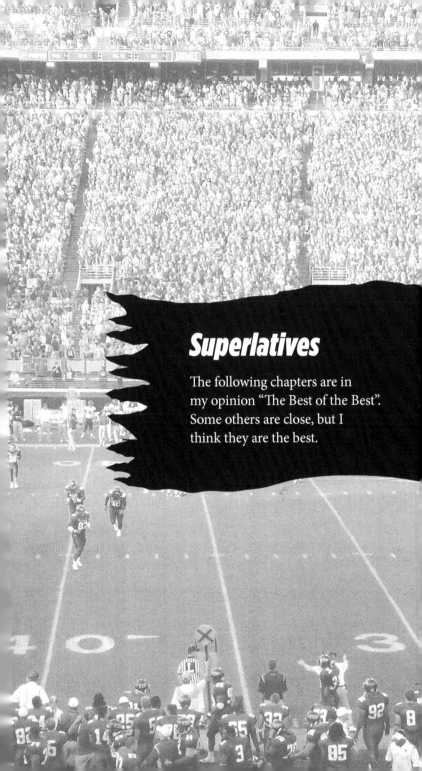

Superlatives

The following chapters are in my opinion "The Best of the Best". Some others are close, but I think they are the best.

ECU Athletics

Best Head Coach

Having seen so much Pirate football I have seen a lot of coaches, starting with Coach Stas. After much thought and debate, in my opinion the best head coach at East Carolina in the last sixty years was Skip Holtz. It's hard to compare coaches from different eras, but Skip Holtz would have very likely been as successful in 1960 as he was almost fifty years later.

Holtz inherited a huge mess in 2005. The Pirates were 3-20 in the two years before he arrived in Greenville. Two wins over Army and a 2-point win over Tulane was all the success the Pirates could find in 2003 and 2004. Many of the losses were blowouts including John Thompson's final game, a 52-14 loss in Charlotte to NC State. Morale was at an all-time low.

Skip Holtz had spent several years in Raleigh when his dad was coaching at NC State, and this helped prepare him for East Carolina. He understood the football culture in the state of North Carolina and he worked hard. He had coached with his father at South Carolina, a school in the same region with a similar culture, and that SEC experience was helpful.

In 2009 Skip's Pirate team went to Tulsa and beat a well-coached team led by the highest-rated quarterback in the country to win the conference championship. It was ECU's first conference championship in thirty-two years.

Holtz not only won a conference championship after many years, he won back-to-back conference championships in C-USA. The second championship was a close win over Houston and future NFL quarterback Case Keenum. Keenum would be named a first team All-American that season and would hold nine NCAA passing records. Holtz played the cards he was dealt in that conference, building his teams to play in C-USA and be competitive in C-USA. ECU has talked about winning championships in every sport. Skip Holtz won championships in football.

In his five seasons with the Pirates, Skip Holtz led the team to four bowl games. The win in the Hawaii Bowl featured Chris Johnson, who broke multiple bowl game records. Holtz's only season without a bowl was his very first year, and that team produced five wins and almost reached bowl eligibility. Either a win at Memphis where the Pirates lost by three points or a win at West Virginia where they fell by five points would have sent them bowling. Holtz is the only coach in ECU history to take his team to four consecutive bowl games. He brought the Pirates back to relevance.

Some people judge college football coaches by players they send to the NFL. Skip Holtz sent four players to the NFL from one team. Three of those players—C.J. Wilson, Jay Ross, and Linval Joseph—earned Super Bowl rings. Linval Joseph played in the NFL for eleven years and was a two-time Pro Bowl selection.

Skip Holtz did an outstanding job interacting with the fans. He was witty and warm and worked well on the speaker's circuit. He fit well into the local Greenville community. The Holtz name was mostly an asset in his years at East Carolina. It was probably a detriment in the end because his name, along with his record, helped recruit him to the University of South

Florida. But the fact is, he left the ECU football program in a much better place than he found it.

It is quite ironic, when you consider the Skip Holtz legacy at East Carolina, realize that there are three former ECU coaches in the ECU Athletics Hall of Fame and all three left East Carolina because they were fired. Skip Holtz is not (yet) a member of the Hall of Fame.

ECU Athletics

Best Assistant Coach

East Carolina has been fortunate to have had a number of truly outstanding assistant coaches—men like Greg Hudson, Cary Godette, Doug Martin, Jeff Jagodzinski, former NFL coach Chuck Pagano, Mark Richt, and some fine current assistants like Donnie Kirkpatrick, Steve Shankweiler, and Blake Harrell.

The best-of-the-best assistant coaches, though, was Lincoln Riley. From Muleshoe, Texas and a former graduate assistant under Mike Leach at Texas Tech, Riley was at East Carolina from 2010 through 2014 and had an amazing effect on the program. In four of his five seasons with the Pirates, ECU participated in a bowl game.

Lincoln Riley's offense put up big numbers. The team records include: the top three seasons for total offense and four of the top five in ECU history, the three best seasons for total passing yardage in ECU history, and the three highest years for points scored per game in ECU history. During several of those years the defense struggled, so his offense didn't always produce the most victories.

In individual games, Riley's teams hold many ECU records including most yards in a single game and most touchdowns in a single game. The Lincoln Riley "Air Raid" offense made for record-setting performances by his players. Both Dominique Davis and Shane Carden set school records playing in the Riley system. Four of his five seasons produced a 1,000-yard receiver, first with Dwayne Harris and later with Justin Hardy. They both went on to play in the NFL. In his final two seasons, he mentored Zay Jones, who holds the ECU and NCAA record for receptions in a single season. Two of Riley's seasons also featured a 1,000-yard rushing performance by a running back. This was a special accomplishment considering the high-octane pass-oriented offense. In 2015 with the loss of quarterback Shane Carden and the leadership of Lincoln Riley, the East Carolina offense would see a 29 percent decrease in offensive yards and would score 137 fewer points. His offense was missed.

Lincoln Riley would be recruited by Bob Stoops to come to the University of Oklahoma as offensive coordinator. In his first season with the Sooners, he would help lead them to the College Football Playoff and he would win the 2015 Broyles Awards as the nation's top assistant coach. This was twelve months after leaving ECU. After another successful season as offensive coordinator, Riley would be named head coach upon the retirement of Bob Stoops. In his five seasons as the Sooner head coach he would have a 55-10 record, win four consecutive Big 12 championships and successfully coach back-to-back Heisman Trophy winners, Baker Mayfield and Kyler Murray. In 2022 he signed a ten-year $110 million contract to coach the USC Trojans. ECU was fortunate to have been a part of his career journey.

ECU Athletics

Best Administrator

Administrators come in all shapes and sizes and they have very different roles, but most people think of the athletic director when they think of administrators. This makes sense, because the AD has the most impact over the athletic programs and the athletic fundraising. In my mind there is one and only one person who literally was head and shoulders above the rest: Michael Terrence Holland. Terry Holland had a more positive impact on East Carolina athletics than any other person in the last 60-plus years.

I first met Terry Holland in 2002 on the night that he was inducted into the N.C. Sports Hall of Fame. I was there to support ECU alumnus Carlester Crumpler, who was inducted that same evening. Terry was witty and engaging that night, which was usually the case. His story about his recruitment to Davidson by Lefty Driesell had the whole room laughing. He told that story many times over the years and it always makes me laugh. I still laugh when I think about it. Our paths would cross again two years later.

Coach Holland was not looking for a full-time administrative job when he was recruited to East Carolina. He wanted to be a consultant. Fortunately, Chancellor Steve Ballard convinced him to take the job as director of athletics with the assurance of strong support from within the athletic department and all over campus. Also, there were family ties to East Carolina. Both his mother and his mother-in-law were alumnae of East Carolina Teachers College. Terry grew up in southeastern North Carolina in Clinton, about eighty miles from Greenville.

To understand Coach Holland it's good to understand the old saying, "People will not remember what you say, but they will always remember how you make them feel." Terry Holland made people feel good. He treated $100 donors like they had given a million dollars.

There was always a quiet confidence with Terry Holland. This may have been a natural ability, or it more likely came from twenty-five years as a basketball coach at a high level followed by twenty years as an athletics director—all prior to coming to Greenville. In those forty-five years in intercollegiate athletics, Holland was exposed to a wide variety of situations. Besides winning more than 400 ACC basketball games as a head coach, coaching in the Final Four, and coaching the national player of the year, he served on and chaired the NCAA basketball committee. His national connections in athletics and respect among his peers were far-reaching. This served him well at ECU.

As a fundraiser, Terry Holland got the job done. He led the campaigns at Virginia to raise $86 million to renovate Scott Stadium and $131 million to build John Paul Jones Arena. He took Virginia to No. 8 in the Director's Cup. At ECU, he expanded Dowdy-Ficklen Stadium with the addition of The Boneyard to increase seating to 50,000. He oversaw fundraising for a new basketball practice facility, new football practice fields, and a new track, finished Clark-LeClair stadium, and directed many other improvements in the athletic campus.

He hired coaches like Skip Holtz, Jeff Lebo and Billy Godwin. He understood that for ECU to be successful and for

ECU fans to be supportive of the program, the Pirates had to regularly play teams they considered rivals. Holland scheduled football games with North Carolina, North Carolina State, Virginia, Virginia Tech, and West Virginia. His relationships with others in the world of intercollegiate athletics made this possible. One of his greatest accomplishments was getting ECU accepted into the American Athletic Conference. This took time and lots of effort. He saw the AAC as a large step up in prestige as well as revenue.

Terry Holland also had a good feel for marketing. He sold ECU as a team with a reach well beyond eastern North Carolina. He used TV ratings from the Raleigh and Charlotte markets to prove that the Pirates' following didn't stop at I-95. He worked hard in those markets to sell the Pirate brand.

Those who worked for him have said that he hired them and let them do their jobs. His philosophy was to hire good people, give them as many resources as he could, and get out of their way. Terry Holland was not a micromanager. He would often seek input from fans and supporters. In the true spirit of college athletics, he also would invite folks from other conferences and teams to come and meet our fans.

He believed in sportsmanship, and one of his few failures came from an attempt to promote sportsmanship. When UNC came to Dowdy-Ficklen Stadium, Coach Holland had promoted the idea that the ECU fans would say in unison, "Welcome….Tar Heels." He seriously underestimated how most fans felt about UNC. It was a weak attempt at best. Most Pirate fans could not choke out those words.

Most importantly, his personality and style were perfect for the culture at East Carolina. Fans would say, "he never sits down," and they were right. At a dinner, a luncheon, a banquet or similar gathering, Terry Holland would walk from table to table and person to person and speak to everyone in the room.

No one would leave an ECU event without personally speaking to Coach Holland and shaking his hand. ECU people remember that Terry Holland made them all feel special and appreciated.

Best Player

This is obviously the subject of much debate. First of all, it is very difficult to compare players from different generations. The level of competition has varied widely at ECU over the years. Second, it is very hard to compare offensive versus defensive players. Third, it is almost impossible to compare players at different positions. How do you compare a quarterback, receiver, running back and offensive tackle?

East Carolina has been blessed with some great players on both offense and defense. Again, it is very difficult to even compare our great quarterbacks like Jeff Blake, Marcus Crandell, David Garrard, and Shane Carden. Wide receivers like Zay Jones, Justin Hardy, and Dwayne Harris were all elite. Running backs have made a special mark at ECU with names like Carlester Crumpler, Scott Harley, Earnest Byner and Junior Smith. On defense, players like Robert Jones, Jeff Kerr, Pernell Griffin, and Kevin Monroe were all very talented. Even special teams players need to be considered. Kicker Jake Verity holds the all-time ECU record for points scored. As a punter, Andrew Bayes averaged an incredible 48.1 yards per punt and was a first-team All-American.

While considering all those incredible players, in my opinion East Carolina's best all-time player was Chris Johnson. Everyone saw his great speed and ability to allude tacklers, but CJ was a true multidimensional player. While he is third on the East Carolina all-time rushing yardage list, that does not begin to tell the story. Chris Johnson was an accomplished pass receiver and holds the ECU record for career receptions by a running back and career receiving touchdowns by a running back. As a kickoff returner, he averaged more than 28 yards per return.

The most important statistic that leads to winning football games is scoring. In 2007, Chris Johnson scored 24 touchdowns and 144 total points. Both are ECU records. The next closest player is Leonard Henry with 108 points in a season. In all-purpose yards, he holds the ECU records for the most yards in a game, in a season and in a career. When Chris Johnson left East Carolina, he had set eighteen school records. No one before or since has come close to that many records.

In the 2007 Hawaii Bowl, the rest of the country got to see what Pirate fans had been watching for four years. Johnson set the NCAA bowl record for all-purpose yards with 408 total yards. He had 181 rushing yards before halftime. Skip Holtz said, "I'm the president of the Chris Johnson fan club. I'm his biggest fan. He is one of the hardest workers on this team. He's humble. He works his tail off."

Chris Johnson went on to become a first-team All-American. He was drafted in the first round of the NFL draft by the Tennessee Titans, one of only two Pirates ever drafted in the first round.

East Carolina was only the beginning for Chris Johnson. He moved on to the NFL and made an immediate impact. In his first season he had more than 1,200 yards rushing. In his next five years he would gain more than 1,000 yards each season. In 2009, Johnson would rush for more than 2,000 yards for only the sixth time in NFL history. As he had done at ECU, he was a complete player; in 2009 he set the NFL record for the most yards from scrimmage. That record still stands.

Chris Johnson is ECU's best player for these four reasons among others:

Scoring - 144 points in a single season

All-purpose yards - in a game, a season, and a career

Eighteen school records

First-team All-American and first-round draft pick

Carl Davis

Best Fans

The question always arises about who has the best fans. There are a lot of schools where the fans appreciate football, the traditions, the tailgating and just the atmosphere. The one school where they seem to enjoy the game and welcome opposing fans with the most enthusiasm is the University of Southern Mississippi. It is a special place with very special people.

First of all, Southern Miss is somewhat like ECU, a "directional school" in the shadow of two Southeastern Conference "flagships," Ole Miss and Mississippi State. Their disdain for those schools is similar to the ECU fans' feeling about UNC and NC State. While ECU is much larger and academically offers more than Southern Miss, the football cultures are similar. Their roots are similar as well since the two schools first met on the field in 1951.

For many years, the Golden Eagles struggled to gain prominence. They would take scheduling deals of three or four games for one home game with schools like Alabama and Nebraska. On their field it said, "Anyone, Anytime, Anywhere." They were proud of it and lived it. Although they don't say it, the famous "chip on the shoulder" is very much a part of the Southern Miss football culture.

Southern Miss has a good tailgate atmosphere. Walking through their tailgate lots with a purple shirt on will get you offers of chicken, bourbon, and everything they have to offer. They seem genuinely appreciative that you made the trip to Hattiesburg, Mississippi. They want to talk football and they will surprise you with their knowledge of East Carolina. While at some places, the majority of fans have no idea about the location or history of ECU, at Southern Miss they know you. They know the history and some of the players.

The university does a nice job of recognizing their best players of the past. Many of their former players remain an active part of the program and even host large tailgates in the parking lots where everyone is welcome, even opposing fans.

If there is a second place for great fans, it's in Provo, Utah at BYU. They have a great football history and football tradition. BYU and football dominate the city of Provo.

The fans at BYU want visitors to feel welcome on the campus and in the stadium. While they are not as knowledgeable about ECU, they will constantly stop visitors and ask where you live, are you enjoying Utah and tell us about your school and team. They have "ambassadors," older gentlemen who stand in the seating areas near the visiting fans. Their job is simple: Be ambassadors for BYU. The ambassadors were pleasant and helpful and interacted with the visiting fans. Most of their fans are actually ambassadors, too.

Carl Davis

Best Stadium

It is really difficult to name the best stadium. Like these other categories, people will have their own ideas of what is really the best. Some people like the best view, the best concessions, the best tailgating, the easiest access, etc. It's hard to compare college stadiums with professional stadiums like Lincoln Financial Field and Raymond James Stadium. ECU played bowl games in the old Houston Astrodome, which now sits abandoned with an uncertain future, and the old Fulton County Stadium, which has been torn down. There are stadiums with great history like Navy Marine Corps Memorial Stadium in Annapolis and more notably, Michie Stadium at Army, which was built in the 1920s.

The layouts of various stadiums—features like the location of the student section, location of the band, new towers and suites, and monster video boards—all vary considerably, and the obviously huge sums of money spent on these facilities is staggering.

After hundreds of games and dozens of stadiums, in my opinion, The Sun Bowl in El Paso is the best. It truly looks like it was carved out of the top of a mountain. The stadium was built for Texas Western University, now known as Texas-El

Paso (UTEP). It sits on the western edge of the campus.

The Sun Bowl was built in 1963 specifically for UTEP but has hosted the annual Sun Bowl game since it was built. It has also hosted other events like concerts. The stadium was expanded in 1982 to seat more than 50,000 fans. Its location is a very easy walk to campus and the surrounding neighborhoods.

The reason the Sun Bowl is so special is the setting. With the rugged desert mountains in the background, it is hard not to be awed by the views. The views change during the day as the sun moves across the sky. There are a few stadiums, like Houston, where there is a city backdrop, but the natural view at the Sun Bowl is better. Some fans might argue that, based on the view, Lavell Edwards stadium in Provo, Utah is better. It too is set in the mountains and has a similar mountain view. In my opinion, the way the Sun Bowl is set in the mountains is better; it looks like it was naturally set in place.

Laurie Maloney

Best Pirate

The best Pirate is not necessarily the best athlete. The best Pirate is not necessarily the one who gave the most money. The best Pirate is the one who is the most enthusiastic about the athletes and the university. The best Pirate is always positive and always optimistic. This is often hard to maintain after a bad loss or a bad season.

There are a lot of folks who were or are great Pirates. People like Walter Williams, Mark Meltzer, Don Edwards, and Dave and Gail Englert come quickly to mind. There are literally thousands who are great Pirates and seize every opportunity to support the teams in every sport.

The best Pirate ever is Matt "Big Guy" Maloney. Yes, he is on the staff and an administrator, but he loves the program like no one else. He is the most positive and most optimistic Pirate ever. Even after a bad loss, he says that we will get them next time.

Matt came to ECU in 1990 from Columbia, South Carolina. He was a walk-on swimmer at the University of South Carolina and he interned in the ticket office at USC. He got his masters in sports administration from Ohio University. Matt interviewed here with Dave Hart and Jimmy Bass and took the job. Looking back 30-plus years later, it was probably one of the best hires in East Carolina history.

Big Guy started in sports marketing at East Carolina but moved to the Pirate Club in 1994. He has worked for five different ADs and several interim athletic directors. He has worked well with all of them. Matt has never lost his enthusiasm in more than three decades with the Pirates. In fact, it seems to increase over time.

Like with Terry Holland, Matt Maloney makes everyone feel good and feel appreciated. He always heaps praise on Pirate donors and Pirate athletes. It's a positive, very genuine attitude. People are drawn to Matt because they can see that he is a positive and sincere person.

Matt's favorite Pirate of all time is Walter Williams. Walter was a father figure to Big Guy. There was a genuine love and respect between the two of them for more than two decades.

One of the fun things that Matt did over the years was to host a party in his backyard on the evening of the annual "Meet the Pirates" event. He would cook hundreds of chicken wings. They were just the best. No one could cook wings like Big Guy. Unfortunately, many of the partygoers would feed Matt's dog, Pee Dee, chicken wings. The poor dog would get sick every year.

Matt's wife Laurie has been a big part of Pirate life for all these years. She has been by his side and supportive of the Pirates as well. Laurie is a big part of the arts community in Greenville. Laurie became very frantic, as any wife would, when Matt was injured in New Orleans. Matt and some other Pirates were standing on Canal Street in front of the J.W. Marriott Hotel the night before a game. Someone a floor or two above the street knocked or dropped a glass off the balcony railing. It hit Matt really hard and cut his head. Blood was pouring down his face and Laurie was screaming. Everyone thought he had been seriously injured. In true "Big Guy" spirit, he was calm and tried to reassure her and everyone in the group that everything was fine! Matt was at the game the next day with a large bandage on his head, a story to tell, and a smile on his face.

Matt is always willing to go above and beyond the call of duty. If the student who wears the Pee Dee mascot outfit is unavailable for an event, Matt will put on the gear and he will proudly be Pee Dee the Pirate. If the coaches needed a driver to a Pirate Club event, just call Big Guy. Whatever it takes to help ECU, Matt is ready and willing to do it.

To show the love and affection that Pirate fans have for Matt, several years ago at an auction a number of supporters pooled their money and bought him a golden retriever puppy. They knew that he had lost Pee Dee and this would be a way to say thanks to their friend and fellow Pirate. Needless to say, there was not a dry eye in the place. Buccaneer became the next member of the Big Guy family.

Although there are many great Pirates, it's hard to compare them to Matt "Big Guy" Maloney. He is truly in a class by himself.

Best Game

After attending hundreds of ECU football games, the number one question I get is, "What was the best game?" The quick answer from a lot of fans is the 1992 Peach Bowl. This is because of the opponent, NC State, and the national ranking, along with it being a bowl game with lots of significance. There were some where the Pirates won late in the game in exciting fashion like Tulsa (2010) or VaTech (2008). Then there were memorable games for other reasons like UNC (71-41 in 2014) or NC State (2013) or the Hawaii Bowl (2007). To me for many reasons that extend beyond football and athletics, the best ECU game ever was ECU vs. Miami in 1999. For me personally, it's not close.

This was more than a football game. Many people know it as the Hurricane Floyd game. With billions in damage and lots of people hurting in Eastern NC, this game was about pride and a beginning to the healing process. A number of people in the area thought that the game should not be played and that the money and the energy expended on a football game should be going to relief efforts in the region. At the time, that was a valid argument.

A full moon was shining brightly that night as the ragtag ECU marching band took the field. The band was made up of some regular band members and some band alumni. They wore T-shirts and jeans because their uniforms were on campus and campus was shut down. That night the marching Pirates never looked or sounded better. Many Pirate football alumni were also present at the game, and they sat together on the lower level on the rows directly behind the bench. When things looked bad for the Pirates, they stood and shouted at the players to not give up.

It took a big second half by David Garrard and the Pirates to come from behind and beat the Hurricanes. The national audience on ESPN saw a great football game, but the feeling and the emotion within Carter-Finley Stadium that night was hard to describe.

How ironic, that this game with such significance to a region devastated by the most significant storm of a generation would be a huge win over a team named the Hurricanes. It was a win for East Carolina and a win for the region. Those who were there will never forget that night and the feeling they had as time expired and they knew the Pirates had won. As the fans and players celebrated on the field and the goalposts came down, the fans in the stands couldn't stop their tears of joy. They knew they had seen something very special that night. It was much more than a football game.

Carl Davis

Best Logo

Logos at East Carolina have come and gone over the years. In the '70s the most notable logo was the Pirate with the dagger in his mouth. Fortunately that old logo has made a comeback, connecting the old with the new.

For many years, ECU had no Jolly Roger logo, also known as the skull and crossbones. The Jolly Roger flag dates to the 17th century and was adopted by pirates in the Caribbean. By the 1720s it was in general use by most pirates in the Atlantic. The name Jolly Roger was used by the English. For the ECU Pirates, the Jolly Roger is the best logo.

In the 1990s there was much discussion among Pirate fans about using the Jolly Roger at ECU. A local Greenville store sold unofficial, unlicensed merchandise with the skull and crossbones. This was all without the ECU trademarks. The store was relatively popular and had a loyal following. Like anything that involves change, there were multiple opinions on this subject. The ECU administration was adamantly opposed to the logo, even as a secondary mark. The stated objection was that a symbol that has been used to warn people about poison should not be a university logo. There was a concern that children would be confused or frightened.

A small group of Pirate fans started a petition drive. This group was led by Mike Yorke, Mark Hatcher and several others. The group raised the funds to buy a large flag and a flag pole to be installed on the southwest corner of Dowdy Ficklen Stadium pending approval by the university.

It sounds strange more than twenty years later, but it was a proud moment as the Pirates ran onto the field and the Jolly Roger was finally hoisted in the stadium. The logo was an instant hit and soon found its way into the officially licensed merchandise of the university.

Over the next few years, the Jolly Roger was incorporated into multiple ECU logos. The Jolly Roger is a part of the "Pirate state of mind" logo seen in the middle of the field. It's part of the current ECU logo on helmets and jerseys. It appears that the children were not scared by the appearance of the Jolly Roger.

Chris Nelson

Best Scholarship Given

ECU fans know that there are eighty-five scholarships for Pirate football. They also know that these eighty-five young men are college students. In spite of what happens on Saturdays in the fall, there is a presumption that they are students as well as athletes.

There are many stories of student athletes getting in trouble, not going to class, or making other bad choices. Every fan has a story like this and remembers a failure by a player. It's disturbing to many people that these players are given an opportunity to attend East Carolina and they don't seize that opportunity. It's hard being a student and an athlete, but it is an opportunity. Lots of fans and donors are not pleased that the money they give for athletic scholarships goes to athletes who do not take advantage of this opportunity to earn a college degree. Only 1.2 percent of college football players are drafted into the NFL. With that statistic in mind, we all understand that college players need to prepare themselves for life after football, but some take advantage of their education to boost their future in a truly impressive way.

While there are many student-athletes who over the years have distinguished themselves outside of athletics, there is one that few people know about. His story has been flying well under the radar since his playing days at ECU. We first met him early in his Pirate career. He is originally from Hickory and we met his parents traveling to away games. His high school coach was David Elder at Hickory High School. Coach Elder is a legend at Hickory High. Elder's 1996 team went undefeated and won the state championship.

The best use of a football scholarship is by Chris Nelson. He was a three-year letterwinner at offensive guard. He was a part of three memorable seasons at ECU in 1999, 2000, and 2001 and played for the PIrates in three bowl games. Chris Nelson worked hard on the field and in the classroom and was an outstanding student. He graduated with a double major in chemistry and physics. He continued the education he started at ECU with an MS in medical physics. He traveled to Texas and earned his PhD in medical physics at the University of Texas Health Science Center. After receiving his PhD, Chris did extensive post-doctoral work in medical radiation therapy at five different locations around the country.

All of this prepared Chris Nelson for his current position— teaching and doing research as Associate Professor in the Department of Radiation Physics - Patient Care, Division of Radiation Oncology at the University of Texas MD Anderson Cancer Center. He has published nineteen peer-reviewed articles and more than thirty abstracts in this highly technical field.

Chris Nelson is a great example of an ECU athlete who used the opportunity he was given and has made the most of that opportunity. He is truly giving back and living the ECU motto of "Servire."

ECU Athletics

Best Pirate Storyteller

This category has some competition, mostly from coaches whose experiences recruiting, playing, and working span many years. Often the best storytellers are Southern coaches who played and coached years ago. Coaches like Pat Dye and Ed Emory both were from the old school of coaches and were great storytellers. Also, the "filter" with many of these people is usually tight, but on occasion some good ones get through. Usually when tempers get short, filters can lift.

In my opinion, no one can top the stories and expressions of Coach Steve Logan. Some of the stories are legendary, but the "Loganisms" add to the humor. When he wanted to be entertaining, he could light up a room with stories. His expressions like, "He's so slow he couldn't run through tall grass," and, "Beat them like a rented mule," amused the Pirate faithful for many years. On the difference in talent between teams, he said, "You can't win the Kentucky Derby with a jackass." On trying a player at different positions, he said, "We tried him at tight end and he couldn't catch a cold in the Klondike." "We tried him on defense and he couldn't tackle a fence post in a forty-acre field."

Logan really understood the fans and reminded people often that the word "fan" is short for fanatic. "If you win, you will be tolerated for six-and-a-half days." He hated losing as much as the fans and he especially hated to be second-guessed on his decisions. In 1996, at West Virginia with ten seconds remaining, Logan decided to go for the two point conversion to win the game. It didn't work and the Pirates lost a heartbreaker. Logan took a lot of criticism for that decision when an extra point would have sent the game to overtime. The next week after a good win he said, "You can write this down in big bold letters. We won this game tonight on the LAST play of the game last week. And you write that down. When you are at East Carolina you GO FOR IT or you don't coach at East Carolina or you don't come to East Carolina or you don't play at East Carolina with a weak heart. WRITE IT!"

Classic Steve Logan was the story he told at a banquet before the Liberty Bowl. Stanford president Condoleezza Rice was on the dais with Logan, and he talked about how President Rice had several large ships named in her honor. He added that at East Carolina after a big win, several farmers had named their tractors after the ECU chancellor, "Ole Dick." But when Logan finished his story on how each university educated its students, he said that when leaving the restroom he was asked why he didn't wash his hands, "At East Carolina they teach us not to pee on our hands," he said. It brought the house down, but President Rice was not amused.

Tremayne Smith

Best Student Pirate

Over the years there have been many students who have distinguished themselves by showing school spirit and Pirate pride. There are probably thousands of students who have made an impact on ECU while they were students in Greenville. Normally we think of a university making an impact on students, but sometimes students make an impact on the university. If the university gave out awards for school spirit at graduation, Tremayne Smith would have been the hands-down winner. He did it all in his years at East Carolina, and his level of enthusiasm and energy was off the chart.

He was elected and served as SGA president while getting a double major in political science and music education. Prior to being SGA president he served as SGA treasurer. He was an effective student leader at ECU. His fellow students admired him.

Tremayne was a very active member of the Marching Pirates for four years. He was the most memorable drum major in the history of the band. College football would not really be college football without marching bands. During the pregame show, he would remove his hat and do handsprings down the length of the field. The crowd loved it, and Tremayne loved doing it. The Marching Pirates had a special drum major with Tremayne Smith.

As the first member of his family to attend college, he was proud to represent his family and never forgot what they had done for him. Prior to graduation, he bought extra copies of his diploma and had them framed. He gave one to each of the eleven family members who came to see him graduate. ECU Chancellor Steve Ballard said, "Tremayne Smith is the best example I know of tomorrow's leader."

After leaving East Carolina, he spent one year in Washington working for a US Senator, but then returned to North Carolina. Tremayne wanted to work with students, and he became the band director at Rocky Mount High School. He revitalized a once-proud band program that had suffered a decline. After only one year, he was named Teacher of the Year in Rocky Mount and won the Encore Award, given nationally for exceptional accomplishments with bands.

In 2015, he returned to Washington and politics to work for two different Congressmen in the US House of Representatives. While in DC, he earned a masters degree in political management from George Washington University.

In 2019, Tremayne moved into the private sector at JPMorgan Chase, remaining in Washington where he serves as a vice president. His warm genuine smile and true Pirate spirit confirm Chancellor Ballard's prediction.

Best Pirate Leaders

These are people who have made a real difference at ECU. Some you may recognize and some you may not know.

Finding Pirate People

We Pirates have seen our share of characters in the last twenty-five years. Having served on numerous search committees and evaluation committees, I have seen a lot of crazy things and crazy people.

To many people, it is hard to understand how or why ECU hired someone or fired someone. They can't comprehend how a certain coach or administrator is at ECU or another school. Maybe I can explain what I know and what I have actually seen.

There are three factors in finding coaches, administrators and other leaders:

Who is available at that point in time.

The reputation of ECU and the history of that particular position or the reputation of the supervisor of the position.

Budget. It's much easier to hire great people with an unlimited budget!

On the first point, as far as who is available is concerned, sometimes coaches are perfectly content in their current position. Not all of them are constantly looking to move up. Some have family ties or alumni ties to a particular institution. Some have just landed in a position and don't want to move in the first few years. This type of mobility is obviously very hard on families. In one search, I was asked repeatedly why we didn't hire a different person. The answer is very simple: All the obvious candidates didn't apply for the job. If they are not in the pool then they will not get the job! Many folks are critical of the use of professional search firms, but I am not one of them. Search firms can offer cover to candidates. The candidates can inquire discreetly with the search firm and find out the direction of the search and if there is an opportunity for them. There is also the question of confidentiality. If someone has a good, high-paying position as a coach or athletic director, they generally do not want their current school to know that they are looking at something else.

The second part is even more important. That is the reputation and view of the position and everything around it. For example, if a well-liked administrator has been forced out of the job, anyone who is applying is going to have that information. It will not be a secret they were forced out, even if they "retired" and were not fired. These positions are not in a vacuum. An athletic director at East Carolina would likely come from a group of 200 to maybe 300 potential applicants. That includes ADs at smaller institutions and assistant administrators at larger institutions. The same numbers are true for coaches. To think that a possible candidate at another school did not know the politics at East Carolina or any other school is naïve. These people talk to each other. They compete with each other. They attend conferences and meetings with each other. They may not personally know a lot about ECU and our programs, but they know someone who does. This is a very small industry and like other small industries, the news, good and bad, spreads quickly. From that group of 200 to 300, you have to eliminate those not looking to move or those who aren't the right fit for other reasons. The real number becomes just a fraction of that.

The third and most obvious factor is salary. While it is true that most of the time you get what you pay for, sometimes you get lucky. This is especially true of up-and-coming talent. We all hate it when a talented young coach moves on and moves up, but the reality is that it is better to lose a successful coach than to have a coach that no one wants. The revenue of the program generally determines what a school can pay to hire or retain a coach. Assistant coaches are very much a part of this equation.

We often hear, "Why don't we hire an ECU person?" That's always a valid question and it has many answers. Did any ECU people apply for the job? If so, were they qualified? My philosophy is to always hire the most qualified person no matter where they went to school. If it's close or if it's a tie between candidates, it should go to the ECU person. They will likely be more invested and know more on the first day.

Sometimes when we are wearing our purple glasses, we tend to not think about many of these important factors. If we put ourselves in these positions, it is easy to see. First, is our family willing to move yet again? Is Greenville an attractive place for them? If I don't get the job, what is that going to do to my current relationship? Is my new potential supervisor in a strong position or maybe on the way out? Is my current situation long term? If I apply, is there an internal candidate who is going to get the job anyway? And for the most competitive, what are the chances we have of being successful with the tools that I will be given? These positions, all the way up to the chancellor, have a risk-versus-reward relationship. Once you weigh all these factors, most of the time, you end up with a very, very small pool of real candidates.

Over the years many people, not directly playing or coaching, have made significant contributions to the Pirate football program. Some are unsung heroes who have made things better without the average fan knowing that they have been a part of this collective effort. Some are well known, some are not.

Matt Maloney

Walter Williams

Every Pirate knew Walter Williams, or at least saw his name on buildings and projects. Few people loved ECU more than Walter Williams. Back in the '90s when Walter was the president of the Pirate Club, I sent him a note saying that there had been a mistake with my seat assignments. He sent me a handwritten note about the solution to the problem, and at the end it said, "Carl, we are all Pirates, no matter where we sit."

Walter and Marie traveled thousands of miles and gave millions of dollars to support Pirate athletics. Walter loved those who loved the Pirates. He was the first person to thank you for coming to an out-of-town event.

Since his passing in 2018 Walter has left a huge void that will likely never be filled. It's sad to think that future Pirates will never have the opportunity to know him and to share his genuine love of ECU.

Steve Tressler

Paul Clifford

Paul Clifford was the president of the ECU Alumni Association for eleven years. During his tenure the alumni association became a dues-paying organization and greatly increased the involvement of ECU alumni all over the country with athletics and the university as a whole. The alumni association raised millions of dollars during his tenure.

Under his leadership, the alumni association organized events in cities all over the country. There were forty-one regional chapters. He understood the importance of alumni involvement with athletics. There were tailgates attended by hundreds of fans in places like Orlando, Dallas and Annapolis. The alumni association organized travel to away games. Many years later, as recently as 2022, Pirate fans still talk about how well-organized those alumni trips were.

The alumni tailgate that was organized before the home games was a huge success. The prices were very reasonable. There was live music and great food and drink. Many fans made this a part of their game-day experience by having their own tailgate and also attending the alumni tailgate. This was done, not to raise money, but to attract more Pirate alumni and to build relationships.

Paul Clifford is now in charge of the largest dues-based alumni association in the country at Penn State, back in his native state of Pennsylvania, but he still loves the Pirates.

Brian Bailey

Brian Bailey

WNCT's Brian Bailey is one of the faces of ECU athletics. He came to Greenville in 1984 and was promoted to sports director in 1986. Brian has covered a lot of ECU games!

He has never forgotten the importance of ECU athletics to the city and the region. While he wears his purple glasses, he is fair to ECU and the opponents. His excitement about sports, and particularly ECU sports, is very genuine. Sportscasters must walk a fine line with reporting on athletes. It's often hard to tell the story without upsetting someone. Brian Bailey knows how to do that.

Brian has won numerous awards for sports reporting and more importantly for community service. He is probably one of the most familiar faces in athletics in eastern North Carolina.

ECU Athletics

Susie Glynn

What would ECU athletics be without cheerleaders and a mascot? Something important would be missing.

Susie Glynn came to school at ECU thirty-five years ago, and of course she was a cheerleader for the PIrates. In 2002 she took on the task of leading the East Carolina cheerleaders. She has best been described as "everyone's mom," but both of her daughters have actually cheered for the Pirates.

She travels with the cheerleaders and the mascot to all the football games. Her schedule is packed with practices and games in multiple sports. Not only is Susie a mom and a coach, she is a full-time teacher in the Pitt County Schools.

In 2021, for the first time in school history, the East Carolina University cheerleading team won the National Cheerleaders Association collegiate championship. It was a huge honor and the result of years of hard work by Susie and the cheerleaders, not only those on the 2021 team, but those cheering for the PIrates in the years leading up to the competition in Daytona Beach.

Susie Glynn is the only ECU coach with a purple mailbox and a purple front door.

ECU Athletics

JJ McLamb

"Mr. Flexible" is the best way to describe JJ McLamb. JJ is an ECU alumnus from the Class of 2001. He started working in athletics almost immediately, starting with a four-year stint as assistant athletics director for operations. His focus was on the many facilities at ECU, from the football stadium to the swimming pool. He also oversaw game-day operations, and that's when things really get busy.

In 2006, he joined former ECU athletic director Mike Hamrick at UNLV. He only stayed a year in Las Vegas before returning to his alma mater. JJ is currently the Executive Associate Athletic Director/Internal Operations. He provides oversight of operations, equipment, video services, strength and conditioning, and grounds and construction projects.

His role is to handle literally hundreds of small details, from making sure the umpires have what they need at a baseball game to getting inspections during multimillion dollar construction projects. He is an unsung hero who must coordinate between teams and officials and handle issues like weather delays and broken play clocks. JJ McLamb has done this quietly and correctly for more than twenty years.

Jeff Connors

Jeff Connors

The strength coach plays an important role in any football program, in part because the strength coach works with the players all year round. Because of the time spent with training and conditioning, his relationship with the individual players is often closer than that of the other coaches.

Jeff Connors was recruited to East Carolina from Bucknell University by Dave Hart. His first stint at ECU began in 1990 under coaches Bill Lewis and Steve Logan. He would join John Bunting at UNC in 2001. Conners remained there until 2011 before returning for a second time to East Carolina, where he worked until his retirement in 2019.

His years with the Pirates were noted for the strength and conditioning records set by his players. More importantly, those years were memorable for the fourth quarter conditioning of the football team. At the end of the game, no one was in better condition than ECU. There was a lot of pride in the fact that no one would outwork the Pirates.

Jeff Connors is well-known around the country among strength coaches, and he is a noted speaker on strength training. He has trained multiple NFL players as well as professional athletes in sports other than football.

Don Edwards

Don Edwards

The University Book Exchange (UBE) opened more than fifty years ago in downtown Greenville. Don Edwards' father started the company when the book business was an important part of a college town, and at that time the logo college merchandise business was just a fraction of the operation.

For more than thirty years, Don has managed the business and has changed as the market has changed. He has been a loyal supporter of ECU athletics in all sports. UBE is a celebration of all things ECU. From the steps with names of Hall of Fame Pirates to the statue of Pee Dee that greets you at the door, University Book Exchange is a Greenville landmark.

Don Edwards has been a major player in the development of the downtown area. His vision is for Greenville to be, in his words, "a great college town." Few people have been as committed for so long to the development of the campus environment. He has shown a willingness to preserve historic buildings to enhance the atmosphere. He believes the success of downtown is closely tied to the success of East Carolina.

Carl Davis

Steve Whetzel

When it comes to looking like a "real" Pirate, no one can top Steve Whetzel. He is known to Pirate Nation as Pirate Steve or Steve the Pirate. He began his role at ECU in 2009 when he first appeared in the team entrance. Since then his role has changed very little. He appears from out of the purple smoke during the playing of "Purple Haze." The ECU team entrance is almost always mentioned among the best in all of college football.

Whetzel is a member of the Shadow Players Stage Combat Group and serves as the artistic and managing director. He joined the group in 2001 and travels the East Coast performing at fairs and festivals. He has been a fight choreographer and he teaches stage combat. He first appeared at Greenville's PirateFest in 2005, which is where he caught the attention of ECU folks.

Fittingly enough, Steve the Pirate lives in Raleigh in a historic building loaded with Pirate artifacts. He studies history and tries to recreate the historic age of piracy. Whetzel often is found in Greenville at other events. He looks and acts the part.

Last Play of the Game: Overtime

Pirate football has come a long way from its humble beginning in 1932 and those first forty years. Most of the teams we played in those years have either abandoned football or are playing at the same level of competition that they were playing back then, but we have been fortunate to schedule teams that have helped to raise our national profile. Through legislative arm twisting, we have been able to schedule our in-state rivals. Most younger fans have only known the East Carolina of the Logan years or the McNeill era. They expect 50,000 fans on a Saturday afternoon and for the Pirates to dominate "lesser" opponents., but lesser opponents may not be what they seem. As a former ECU coach once said, "The other team wants to win, too." For the football program to sustain itself, ECU must play teams that our fans want to see, and we must win more than we lose.

East Carolina has been fortunate to have had some strong leadership both as coaches and in other leadership roles. We have been fortunate to also have loyal fans, alumni, and donors. ECU has had support from Greenville and the entire region. It's natural that there have been ups and downs with leaders and the football program in our ninety-year history.

It's not realistic to think otherwise. For the Pirates, it has been mostly a good history.

Our future in football, in all athletics and with the entire university, lies with leadership. With the changing landscape in college athletics, we must hope that our leaders have built the relationships and have the vision to make ECU all it can be.

I have been fortunate to have seen it for many years from many seats in many different places. That's my view from twenty rows up.

Carl Davis

About the Author

Carl Davis has been an observer of ECU football for more than sixty years. He has been involved with the university since his days as a student. He has served as chairman of the East Carolina University Board of Visitors, chairman of the East Carolina University Alumni Association Board of Directors, as a member of the East Carolina University Foundation Board, and as a member of the ECU Athletics Hall of Fame Committee. In 2014, he received the Distinguished Service Award for service to ECU.

His professional career has revolved around the radio and television industry. For fourteen years he was the assistant general manager at UNC-TV. He is a member of the North Carolina Association of Broadcasters Hall of Fame.

Carl and his wife Martha now live in Greenville, North Carolina after more than forty years in Raleigh.

Made in the USA
Columbia, SC
18 July 2023

20596212R00143